UNIVERSITY OF NORTH CAROLINA
STUDIES IN THE ROMANCE LANGUAGES AND LITERATURES
Number 46

THE POETIC ART OF
JUAN DEL VALLE CAVIEDES

THE POETIC ART OF
JUAN DEL VALLE CAVIEDES

BY
DANIEL R. REEDY

CHAPEL HILL
THE UNIVERSITY OF NORTH CAROLINA PRESS

DEPÓSITO LEGAL: V. 166 — 1964

PRINTED IN SPAIN

ARTES GRÁFICAS SOLER, S. A. — VALENCIA — 1964

To my wife and daughter

TABLE OF CONTENTS

		Page
PREFACE		11

PART I

			Page
		Caviedes' Epoch, Life, Works, and Critics ...	15
Chapter	I.	Historical and Literary Currents	15
—	II.	Life and Works	19
—	III.	The Poet and His Critics	29

PART II

			Page
		Analysis of Poetic Works	41
—	IV.	Forms of Amorous Poetry	49
—	V.	Forms of Poetry of Social Satire	60
		A. Medical Satire	60
		B. Satire of Other Professions and of Types ...	83
		C. Feminine Satire	93
—	VI.	Forms of Religious Poetry	110
—	VII.	Miscellaneous Poems	127
—	VIII.	Conclusion and Evaluation	145
APPENDIX I			150
APPENDIX II			158
LIST OF WORKS CONSULTED			166

PREFACE

The material contained in this study of the poetic art of Juan del Valle Caviedes represents in part the result of more than four years of active interest in the works of this seventeenth century poet, who spent most of his life in the Viceroyalty of Peru, although he was born on the Peninsula. For a number of reasons, which will be brought out later, Caviedes' poetic production remained in near oblivion for a period of almost two centuries; however, interest in the poet and his significance in the development of Spanish American colonial letters has shown a marked increase during the past three or four decades. This study, then, is largely a result of the present writer's interest in Peruvian letters in general, and the pre-revolutionary period in particular. It is firmly believed that Caviedes' works represent only one of many cases in which modern methods of analysis, criticism, and evaluation can serve to broaden the perspectives or scope of this specific country's national literature, while at the same time making a contribution on a wider scale to the understanding and appreciation of the whole of Spanish American letters.

The initial portion of the study provides a brief historical, literary, and biographical background of the poet. Attention is also focused on the author's poetic production and on the criticism which has been made of it during the past one hundred years. These factors will then serve as extrinsic materials which, although they are not always necessary for an adequate appreciation of the individual or collective works, enlarge the scope of one's knowledge and understanding of the poet.

In Part II, which is the focal point of this study, the results of an analysis of the poet's works are presented and described as objectively as possible. In most cases the results of the analyses and descriptions are substantiated with the aid of textual citations. The elements which are given particular attention in the analyses are form, including structure and techniques, which make up the author's style, and content, including subject matter, themes, and theses. Since subject matter cannot be completely separated from form or excluded from a study of this type, it, too, is commented upon as an integral part of the description of the poet's art. In addition to these elements, attention is given to some of the salient features of epoch style as evidenced in these poetic works.

Since this work was originally submitted in dissertation form as partial fulfillment of requirements for the Ph. D. at the University of Illinois, I would like to acknowledge the aid of Professor Fred P. Ellison now of the University of Texas, under whose direction it was first conceived, and express my sincere appreciation to Professor Luis Leal of the University of Illinois, under whose guidance the analyses and writing were accomplished. I should also like to extend my thanks to the following to whom I am indebted for aid in obtaining bibliographical material, books, and microfilm: Professor James O. Crosby of the University of Illinois; Professor Pedro Benvenutto Murrieta of the Universidad Nacional Mayor de San Marcos; don W. Jaime Molíns of Buenos Aires; Biblioteca Nacional de Lima; Biblioteca Nacional de Madrid; Yale University Library; Duke University Library; and the Library of the University of Illinois. Finally, I am indebted to my colleagues, Professors John Esten Keller and Nicholson B. Adams, whose aid and suggestions have helped to improve this study, and to the University Research Council of the University of North Carolina which has made the publication of this work possible.

PART I

CAVIEDES' EPOCH, LIFE, WORKS, AND CRITICS

Chapter I

HISTORICAL AND LITERARY CURRENTS

While the seventeenth century had seen a gradual decline in Spain's political and economic fortunes, such was not necessarily the corresponding case in her overseas possessions, for outwardly at least it was a period of growth in material wealth and population.[1] By the end of the century most of the colonial possessions were becoming more self-sufficient and less dependent on the mother country. Peru's greatest wealth continued to come from her mines, especially those at Potosí and Huancavelica, and the *quinto real* was still sent regularly to the reigning monarch in the Peninsula. Lima's growth had been phenomenal during the century and by 1700 showed an increase of 29,972 persons, a growth of almost three hundred percent since the last census in 1600.[2]

All was not Utopian, however, for the Pacific coast was infested with pirates during the last half of the century and they proved to be one of the major problems confronting the various viceroys. One pirate, Edward Davis, raided the coast of the Viceroyalty repeatedly from 1683 until 1687 when he and his cohorts

---

[1] Caviedes' "Quintillas en el certamen que se dio por la Universidad, a la entrada del Conde de la Monclova. Fue un coloquio que dos pobres de las gradas tuvieron, celebrando la abundancia de mantenimientos que con su govierno había y llorando la esterilidad de tiempos pasados" gives some insight into the improvement of economic conditions in Peru during the last quarter of the seventeenth century. See *Obras de don Juan del Valle y Caviedes*, ed. Rubén Vargas Ugarte (Lima, 1947), pp. 40-43.

[2] Manuel de Mendiburu, *Diccionario histórico-biográfico del Perú* (Lima, 1885), VI, 541.

were finally beaten off under the leadership of the Virrey Conde de la Palata. The economy and life of the city were so disrupted for a number of years that it was finally decided to raise a wall around Lima as a fortification, a task which was accomplished from 1684 to 1687 at a cost of over 500,000 pesos. [3]

Piracy was not the only problem in Lima during Caviedes' lifetime. The earthquakes which lasted intermittently from October 20 to December 2, 1687, had a profound effect on the life and economy of the City. [4] Few buildings were left standing after they ended. Vargas Ugarte in his *Historia del Perú* (1954; p. 414) estimates that the losses in the metropolitan area alone were well over 150,000,000 pesos.

The task of directing the reconstruction of Lima and the establishment of a firm economy fell to the Conde de la Monclova who arrived at Callao in a viceregal capacity on August 15, 1689. [5] Besides the herculean efforts expended in rebuilding Lima, the Viceroy also succeeded in accomplishing another important task. Before the end of the century a stone dock was constructed in the port of Callao. The work was begun in 1693 and was finally finished by May 26, 1696. The total cost of the project was

---

[3] The problems with pirates and the decision to build a wall around Lima are discussed in the poems entitled "Memorial que da la muerte al virrey, Duque de la Palata, en tiempo que se arbitraba enviar navíos y gente para pelear con el enemigo o si se construía muralla para guardar esta Ciudad de Lima" and "Aviendo dicho el doctor Yáñez que se disculpaba de no haber hecho segunda visita a un enfermo por vivir fuera de murallas, estando Lima amagada de corsarios" (*Obras*, pp. 250-252 and 240-241).

[4] The earthquakes which destroyed the City are mentioned in the *romance* "Al terremoto acaecido en Lima el 20 de octubre de 1687", in the sonnet "Al terremoto que asoló esta ciudad" and the *décima* "Al dicho corcobado porque se puso espada luego que sucedió el terremoto de octubre de 1687" (*Obras*, pp. 79-83, 95, and 237). In the *romance* "Aviendo el doctor Melchor Vázquez avecindádose, después de el temblor, en la calle nueva los vecinos no le admitieron y le fijaron este edicto en la esquina", mention is made of the earthquakes and the reconstruction period which followed (*Obras*, pp. 263-264).

[5] The arrival of this viceroy in 1689 is mentioned by the poet in the "Quintillas en el certamen que se dio por la Universidad, a la entrada del Conde de la Monclova" (*Obras*, pp. 40-43).

approximately 155,000 pesos, but its completion was celebrated by all Lima as one of the greatest achievements of the century. [6]

The Church still held a heavy hand over the political as well as the intellectual life of the Viceroyalty. Felipe Barreda y Laos in his *Vida intelectual de la colonia* (1909; p. 190) has noted that the rivalry between the *colegios* of the various religious orders became so strong that the University of San Marcos was entering a period of decadence, with the result that intellectual and literary life outside the realm of the Church was somewhat stifled. In politics, don Melchor de Liñán y Cisneros, the Archbishop of Lima, was named Viceroy in 1678 and held that position until 1681 when the Duque de la Palata arrived. Although the Inquisition had not held a single public *auto de fe* since 1667, on March 16, 1693, it was resolved to have one in the Church of Santo Domingo. This was followed by another a year later in the same site, but there were no public burnings and the people involved were given either corporal punishments or terms in jail.

Insofar as the literary world of the epoch is concerned, one finds only a limited number of writers of importance in the Peruvian Viceroyalty. Although much was written in prose by theologians who wished to recount miracles which had occurred in the New World, some works in verse did appear. The Jesuit Rodrigo de Valdés' *Poema histórico sobre la fundación y grandezas de Lima* (1687) in both Spanish and Latin was a kind of prelude to Pedro de Peralta Barnuevo's *Lima fundada,* which was not to appear until the next century in 1732. It was not in coastal Lima that the century's most outstanding prose work was to be written, but in the Andean town of Cuzco. A *cuzqueño,* Juan de Espinosa Medrano, nicknamed El Lunarejo, began his literary career at the early age of fourteen with dramatic pieces, but the work which is most often associated with his name is the *Apologético en favor de Góngora.* According to one critic it is the most important work in Peruvian prose after the Inca Garcilaso's *Comenta-*

---

[6] One of the last happenings in the century that is mentioned by Caviedes is the construction of the dock at Callao. The work is the subject of three different sonnets, "Al muelle que hizo en el Callao Monclova", "Al muelle acabado", and "Al mismo asunto del muelle" (*Obras,* pp. 102-103).

rios reales. [7] It is really after El Lunarejo's death in 1688 that Caviedes' importance in Peruvian letters begins to rise and it is only eclipsed by a single contemporary, Pedro de Peralta Barnuevo, who outlived him by more than a half century. It must be noted, however, that the latter's literary works belong predominantly to the first three decades of the eighteenth century and not to the period of Caviedes' maximum creativity. In a strict sense there was no single writer in poetry or prose to challenge Caviedes' place as a literary figure in the Viceroyalty during the last quarter of the seventeenth century.

The other great seat of colonial culture during this time was the viceregal capital, Mexico, where two of Caviedes' contemporaries lived and wrote. The savant Carlos de Sigüenza y Góngora is more often remembered for his intellectual attainments in science and astronomy than he is for his literary productions. The other, a woman and poetess whom Caviedes admired greatly, was Sor Juana Inés de la Cruz. Many parallels may be drawn between these two. Their lives coincide almost exactly insofar as dates are concerned, while both were the central literary figures in their respective seats of culture in the New World. However, their formal education was quite different and there are certainly as many contrasts between the two as there are parallels. There is no question, though, that the literary position held by the poetess in the second half of the seventeenth century in Spanish America is unrivaled, and even a person who feels considerable admiration for Caviedes' works could not challenge this fact. Nonetheless, Caviedes' place of importance as a poet in his epoch is second only to that of the *monja mexicana,* although for numerous reasons which will be pointed out later, it has never been accorded him wholeheartedly except by a limited number of critics and literary historians. Surely there was no other poet during the second half of the seventeenth century in Spanish America, except Sor Juana, who challenged his position of importance.

---

[7] Ventura García Calderón, "La literatura peruana (1535-1914)", *Revue Hispanique,* XXXI (1914), 325-326.

CHAPTER II

LIFE AND WORKS

For almost one hundred years a kind of fictional aura has surrounded the details of Caviedes' life. This has been due primarily to the early biographical sketch of the poet made by don Ricardo Palma in the prologue to Manuel de Odriozola's edition of Caviedes' works in 1873.[1] According to Palma, a manuscript containing biographical notes in an *hoja suelta* was in his possession in 1859, but was shortly thereafter stolen. In the notes there were enough facts to enable the *tradicionista* to compose a biography of the poet. Needless to say the notes that Palma mentions have never been seen since that time. In truth the entire idea smacks of the characteristic techniques which Palma used quite often in his *Tradiciones peruanas*. According to this apocryphal biography, Caviedes was born in Lima, the son of a rich merchant. At the age of twenty he first went to Spain and returned three years later. Finding himself in possession of a sizeable fortune, the poet supposedly embarked on a carefree life of pleasure and did not begin to write poetry until about 1681. With his wealth almost spent, he married and invested his remaining funds in a small shop on the banks of the river Rímac which flows around Lima, hence the *apodo* of Poeta de la Ribera. Palma continues that after becoming a widower, Caviedes turned to drink and died of alcoholism in 1692.

---

[1] Ricardo Palma, "Prólogo muy preciso," in *Documentos literarios del Perú*, ed. Manuel de Odriozola (Lima, 1873), V, 5-8.

Nothing could be much farther from the true facts, which have since come to light, than the totally fictitious biography created by don Ricardo Palma. However, the nickname of Poeta de la Ribera and these false biographical facts were quoted by many, from Menéndez y Pelayo in the *Antología de poetas hispanoamericanos* to Luis Alberto Sánchez in his *Poetas de la colonia*, until 1937, when the Peruvian scholar Guillermo Lohmann Villena published an article entitled "Dos documentos inéditos sobre Juan del Valle y Caviedes" in the *Revista Histórica* of Lima.[2]

The documents that were brought to light were Caviedes' marriage contract dated in 1671 and his last will and testament from 1683. According to the facts contained in these records, he was actually born in the town of Porcuna, province of Jaén in Andalusia. The exact date of his birth has not yet been discovered, since the parish priest of the church of Nuestra Señora de la Asunción of Porcuna has failed to turn up such evidence in the parish archives.[3] Various tentative dates of birth have been suggested, but all of them are entirely conjectural.[4] Caviedes was evidently born around the middle of the century, but there is no basis for the establishment of a precise date. According to the poet's testimony at the time of his marriage, he was the legitimate son of Don Pedro del balle Cabiedes and Doña María de Cabiedes who were both from Porcuna. A subsequent search for either their baptismal or marital records in the church of Porcuna has resulted in no additional information about them.[5]

Exactly when Caviedes came to the New World is yet another mystery, although it was learned in 1944, with the discovery of

---

[2] Guillermo Lohmann Villena, "Dos documentos inéditos sobre Don Juan del Valle y Caviedes," *Revista Histórica*, IX (1937), 277-283.

[3] Guillermo Lohmann Villena, "Un poeta virreinal del Perú: Juan del Valle Caviedes," *Revista de Indias*, no. 33-34 (1948), 771-794.

[4] The earliest birth date, the 1630's, is suggested by Lohmann Villena, "Un poeta virreinal...," p. 777, and the latest, 1655, by Luis Alberto Sánchez, "Un Villón criollo," *Revista Iberoamericana*, II (April, 1940), 81. The most commonly cited date is 1652.

[5] Lohmann Villena, "Un poeta virreinal...," pp. 777-778.

his "Carta ... a la monja de México...", that this happened early in his youth. He says:

> De España pasé al Perú
> tan pequeño, que la infancia
> no sabiendo de mis musas,
> ignoraba mi desgracia. [6]

Besides these facts no other knowledge of his journey to the Peruvian Viceroyalty has yet been discovered. A search in the registers of the Casa de la Contratación, now the Archivo General de las Indias, has not served to clarify this mystery. [7] It is known, however, that the poet was not alone and friendless on his arrival in Lima. A cousin, don Tomás Berjón de Caviedes, was a man of considerable influence who before the end of the century held the posts of Alcalde, Fiscal, and finally Oidor of the Audiencia de Lima. [8] The fact that the poet was a cousin of Tomás Berjón de Caviedes was established through the former's *testamento* in which he mentions Doña Thomasa, his cousin's wife, as one sees in the following passage from that document:

> yten deClaro que a un Caxonero nombrado P° del aguila que biue en frente de la peña oradada le tengo empeñada una sortixa de diamantes en quarenta ps. la qual dha. sortixa es de mi S^{ra} Dª Thomasa Verxon de Cauiedes que me la dio para que la empeñasse en veyntidos ps. Y yo la empeñe hasta en quarenta que la dha. mi prima le pida y me perdone por Dios la demacia y que la saque del dho. caxonero. [9]

Besides these relatives, no knowledge of others has come to light to the present.

What Caviedes' means of livelihood consisted of is still another conjecture. From what he says in the following passage

---

[6] Guillermo Lohmann Villena, "Una poesía autobiográfica de Caviedes inédita," *Boletín Bibliográfico de la Universidad Nacional Mayor de San Marcos*, XIV (June, 1944), 100-102.

[7] Lohmann Villena, "Un poeta virreinal...," p. 778. See note no. 6 of this source.

[8] Lohmann Villena, "Dos documentos inéditos...," pp. 277-278.

[9] *Ibid.*, p. 281.

from the "Carta", it is believed that he was possibly involved in mining:

> Héme criado entre peñas
> de minas, para mí avaras,
> mas, ¿cuándo no se complican
> venas de ingenio, y de plata? (*Obras*, p. 34).

It is known for a fact, however, that he was connected in some way with mining, since a "Protocolo de Carlos de Arengo" found in the Archivo Nacional de Lima mentions a mine that was discovered by Caviedes in Huarochirí.[10]

According to the marriage contract and the testament, Caviedes was married on March 15, 1671, to doña Beatriz de Godoy Ponce de León, a native of the town of Moquegua. The ceremony took place in the Cathedral of Lima and was performed by the Licenciado don Juan de la Barreda, a priest from the church of San Lorenzo de Quinti. The couple subsequently had five children, all of whom are mentioned in the poet's will. They were Antonio, Pedro, Juan, María Josefa, and Alonso. Their fates remain unknown to the present. Since the surname, Caviedes, still exists in Peru, it might be wistfully conjectured that they lived and were the ancestors of the present people who bear the name. At any rate it does not appear that any one of them was famous or infamous enough to warrant a record of his life; at least no information has yet been brought to light.

Caviedes' testament, which was dated as March 26, 1683, is the only other document which contains much information about the satirist's life. As one sees in the will, he undoubtedly thought his time had come:

> Sepan quantos esta carta de mi testamento última y postrimera voluntad vieren como yo Don Ju° del Valle y Cauiedes ... estando enfermo de la enfermedad que Dios nro. Sr. ha sido seruido darme y en mi entero Juicio y creiendo como firme y Verdaderamente creo en el myste-

---

[10] Lohmann Villena, "Un poeta virreinal...," p. 283. See note no. 1 of this source.

rio de la Santissima trinidad p^e hixo y espiritu Santo tres personas distintas y Un solo Dios uerdadero... [11]

He continues by saying that he wishes to be buried in the habit of San Francisco and if he dies in the Hospital de San Andrés, he wishes to be placed in its burial plot. The rest of the will clearly shows that he was far from being a wealthy man. A long list of debts owed to a number of people is given and he asks that they be paid by giving them his personal possessions. All other goods are left to doña Beatriz who is also appointed the guardian and tutor of their infant children.

Caviedes did not die on that occasion, however, and though little is known of him from that time until his death, some of his poems testify to his continued presence in the Viceroyalty until at least 1696. He wrote of the earthquake which occurred on October 20, 1687; his "Diálogo entre Portugués y Bachán" mentions the arrival of the Conde de la Monclova, Peru's twenty-third viceroy, who entered Lima on August 15, 1689; a sonnet to Dr. Bermejo appeared in print in 1694;[12] and finally the sonnet "Al muelle acabado," referring to the dock built under the direction of the Conde de la Monclova, leaves no doubt that the poet was still alive as late as 1696 or even 1697.

Death did come, nonetheless, during the intervening period between 1696 and 1700, since the records of the census of Lima at the turn of the century fail to show proof of his existence.[13] As far as his last years are concerned, they were evidently not all happy ones. The *endechas* "A la muerte de mi esposa" tell of his anguish and affirm the fact that he was left a widower sometime after 1683. Also, Lohmann Villena has found an unpublished letter in the Bibliothèque National of Paris which asserts that the poet became deranged in his last days and ran naked through the streets of Lima and the fields outside the city.[14] In truth it seems a tragic end of life for anyone, but it is also somewhat

---

[11] Lohmann Villena, "Dos documentos inéditos...," p. 279.

[12] Hermilio Valdizán, *Apuntes para la bibliografía médica peruana* (Lima, 1928), pp. 38-39. The sonnet was included in the publication of Dr. Bermejo's "Discurso de la enfermedad de sarampión...," which was published in 1694.

[13] Lohmann Villena, "Un poeta virreinal...," p. 780.

[14] *Idem.* See note no. 12 of this source.

ironic, since after so many years of making people laugh at others, he should become the laughing-stock of those about him.

Perhaps one of the reasons that Caviedes' works have been so little studied or commented on until the past two decades is due to the fact that there were no editions published until more than one hundred fifty years after his death. The first attempt to collect and publish a sizeable portion of his poems was made by Manuel de Odriozola in 1873, with the aid of don Ricardo Palma, in volume V of his important *Documentos literarios del Perú*. As will be seen later, other selections were published in the intervening period between that date and 1947, when Rubén Vargas Ugarte presented what he termed the *Obras de Don Juan del Valle y Caviedes*.

Manuscripts of the poet's works did circulate during his lifetime and copies of some of them are still in existence. Of the eight manuscripts known at the present, two are located in the Yale University Library; two others are in the Biblioteca Nacional de Lima; a fifth copy is to be found in the Biblioteca Nacional de Madrid; a sixth is in the Duke University Library; a seventh copy is in the Biblioteca del Convento de San Francisco in the mountain town of Ayacucho, Peru; and an eighth is in the private collection of don W. Jaime Molíns of Buenos Aires. These eight constitute the only manuscripts of Caviedes' works actually known to be in existence at the present. Copies in microfilm have been obtained of all the manuscripts except the one at Ayacucho. To more easily identify these manuscripts in the text of the present study, they have been given the arbitrary titles of MSS. Yale-A, Yale-B, Lima-A, Lima-B, Madrid, Duke, Ayacucho, and Molíns. Subsequent references will be made to them as identified above. [15]

While manuscripts of Caviedes' works were circulating in colonial Lima at the end of the seventeenth century, there were few cases of the poet's works being put in print. It is not surprising, however, when one considers the lewd and near pornographic nature of a few of them and the acrimonious satire of many of the poet's contemporaries who were people of considerable social and

---

[15] See Appendix II of this study for a more detailed examination and description of these different MSS.

political position. It might well be imagined that Caviedes felt safer by passing copies of his manuscripts around clandestinely, rather than attempting to publish his poems in quantity. Too, it must be noted that many of the works printed in that epoch were more often of a religious or doctrinal nature than they were poetic and they were subject to ecclesiastic and governmental censure. At any rate only three of Caviedes' poems were published during his lifetime. The first to be put in print was the "Romance en que se procura pintar y no se consigue: La violencia de dos terremotos, conque el Poder de Dios asoló esta Ciudad de Lima, Emporeo de las Indias occidentales y la más rica del mundo," which appeared about 1688, or one year after the second of the two great earthquakes that practically destroyed Lima.[16]

The second of Caviedes' individual poems to appear was the "Quintillas en el certamen que se dió por la universidad, a la entrada del Conde de la Monclova. Fué un Coloquio que dos pobres de las gradas tuvieron, celebrando la abundancia de mantenimientos que con su govierno había y llorando la esterilidad de tiempos pasados." The poem appeared as an addendum to an "Oración panegírica..." that was published in Lima in 1689.[17]

The only other poem by Caviedes to be published during his lifetime was an untitled sonnet attached to the famous "Discurso de la enfermedad de sarampión..." by Dr. Francisco Bermejo y Roldán.[18] The poem begins "Créditos de Avicena, gran Bermejo" and is undoubtedly by the author. It has not appeared, however, in any of the editions of his works, nor is it included in any of the manuscripts.

Almost a century passed before interest in the poet was strong enough to warrant the publication of a few isolated poems in the *Mercurio Peruano* by Hipólito Unánue, who wrote under the pen name of "Aristio." The first of them, which appeared in the April 28, 1791 issue, was the *décima* "Al dicho corcobado porque se puso

---

[16] José Toribio Medina, *La imprenta en Lima (1584-1824)* (Santiago, 1904), II, 178-179.
[17] *Ibid.*, pp. 180-181.
[18] Valdizán, pp. 38-39.

espada luego que sucedió el terremoto de octubre de 1687."[19] A second poem "A un doctor que trayendo anteojos pronosticó a una señora preñada que pariría hija, y no parió sino hijo" was published in the *Mercurio Peruano* on June 12 of that same year (Vol. II, p. 3). During 1792 two more of Caviedes' poems appeared in the same magazine. These included the "Conversación que tuvo con la muerte un médico, estando enfermo de riesgo" and the "Respuesta de la muerte al médico" (Vol. V, pp. 152 and 156). Had it not been for these samples offered in the eighteenth century, Caviedes' works might have remained in oblivion for a much longer time than they did. The *Mercurio Peruano* was the first published magazine in Lima and executed more influence then than it does probably today. It is unfortunate, however, that Unánue did not mention the source of his materials, since it might have given more insight into the manuscript tradition of the works.

One other single poem by the author was published early in the nineteenth century. This was the somewhat lewd "Defensa que hace un pedo al ventoso" which appeared by itself in Lima in 1814. It soon became the poet's most notorious work and served to give him the classification of a pornographic writer.

The real increase in interest in Caviedes' works came in 1873 when Manuel de Odriozola, assisted by Ricardo Palma, published the *Diente del Parnaso* together with *Poesías serias y jocosas* in his important *Documentos literarios del Perú* (Vol. V). Odriozola's edition was far from complete, since it contained only one hundred thirty-nine poems, slightly more than half of the total known works. The most conspicuous absence was that of the entire group of religious poems which evidently did not form a part of the manuscript used for the edition. It was, nevertheless, a monumental first step toward a better understanding of Caviedes' stature as a poet and the artistic merits of the individual works.

At the end of the nineteenth century, when interest in Caviedes' works began to increase, Ricardo Palma published another edition of the poet's works together with the *Actas* of the *Tertulia* of the Marqués Castell dos Rius in a single volume entitled *Flor*

---

[19] Hipólito Unánue, "Rasgos inéditos de los escritores peruanos," *Mercurio Peruano*, I (April 28, 1791), 312-313.

de Academias y Diente del Parnaso (1899). In his prologue to the latter he says:

> Ya en 1873, en muy incorrecta edición, habíamos dado a conocer las producciones de Caviedes que, hasta aquel año, permanecían inéditas. Hoy, teniendo a la vista un manuscrito que perteneció a la librería Zegarra, hemos hecho algunas correcciones sustanciales. (p. 335)

It is difficult to point out exactly what corrections were made by Palma in the edition. He includes only one hundred four compositions (thirty-five less than the *Documentos literarios*) and the only apparent changes are in the titles of some of the poems.

Luis Alberto Sánchez and Daniel Ruzo followed Palma's 1899 edition for their publication of the *Diente del Parnaso* in Lima in 1925. It is quite fragmentary and contains only fifty-eight poems, most of which are against doctors. From that time until 1947, only fragments of the poet's works were published in anthologies and articles. Ventura García Calderón published twenty-four selected poems in his 1938 anthology of the *Biblioteca de cultura peruana*;[20] Guillermo Lohmann Villena brought forth "Una poesía autobiográfica" in an article in 1944;[21] while the most substantial contribution was that of Luis Fabio Xammar who in 1945 published twenty-four previously unknown sonnets.[22] In 1946 Herman Hespelt included six of Caviedes' poems in his anthology, but unfortunately only three are definitely by the poet.[23]

Eventually in 1947 Fr. Rubén Vargas Ugarte, a Jesuit professor of history at the Universidad Católica in Lima, prepared an edition

---

[20] Ventura García Calderón, *Biblioteca de cultura peruana: El apogeo de la literatura colonial*, V and *Los místicos*, VI (Paris, 1938), pp. 203-271 and 183 respectively.

[21] Lohmann Villena, "Una poesía autobiográfica...," pp. 100-102.

[22] Luis Fabio Xammar, "Veintitrés sonetos inéditos de Juan del Valle Caviedes," *Fénix, Revista de la Biblioteca Nacional*, no. 3 (1945), 632-641.

[23] *An Anthology of Spanish American Literature*, eds. E. Herman Hespelt et al. (New York, 1946), pp. 73-79. The three poems which belong to Caviedes are the "Coloquio que tuvo con la muerte un médico moribundo," "A mi muerte próxima" and "Cuatro contras que ha de tener el entendido para serlo."

which he intended to be definitive and entitled it the *Obras de Don Juan del Valle y Caviedes*. It is, indeed, the most complete edition yet published, but it suffers from some serious defects. At least twenty known poems are not included. Ten of these have never been published, while a like number were omitted deliberately from a sense of propriety, for he says, "Es casi un deber cribar su obra poética y arrojar a un lado como inútil paja todo cuanto de repulsivo, maloliente o de subido color hallamos en ella".[24] Two other poems are very incomplete and five have been censored and mutilated so as to protect the reader from any indecorous remarks which they contained. A final serious fault of the edition is that the editor arbitrarily picks the poems from any of the manuscripts available to him. No attempt has evidently been made to collate or compare the poems, except in a few isolated cases, and not a single source for the individual works is given anywhere. A brief perusal of any two manuscripts immediately shows important differences between the versions of a single poem.

Since 1947, at least two important anthologies have included works by Caviedes. They are the *Antología general de la poesía peruana* (Lima, 1957) by Alejandro Romualdo and Sebastián Salazar Bondy which contains thirty-nine poems, and the anthology, *Literatura hispanoamericana* (New York, 1960), by Enrique Anderson Imbert and Eugenio Florit which includes only three.

This survey of the most important editions and appearances of Caviedes' works brings forth some important facts. First of all one see that interest in Caviedes as a poet has been increasing in the last two or three decades as contrasted with the two centuries of near oblivion that he suffered. Also the incompleteness and serious deficiencies of scholarship apparent in these editions point out the necessity for a well-done critical edition of the works of a poet of Caviedes' stature.

---

[24] Rubén Vargas Ugarte, "Introducción," in *Obras de Don Juan del Valle y Caviedes* (Lima, 1947), p. XII.

CHAPTER III

THE POET AND HIS CRITICS

It is unfortunate that most of the available criticism of Caviedes' poetry is limited primarily to generalities which are usually uncorroborated with textual evidence from the works themselves. In most cases the comments are directed toward the biographical problems involved rather than toward the literary aspects of the works. Many of these generalities are so vague and misleading as to give one a distorted picture of the true nature of Caviedes' works. Included in this brief review of the poet's critics are those which in some way have contributed significantly to a better understanding of the works through objective criticism rather than impressionistic generalities.

The first concerted effort to describe Caviedes' works and discuss their relative importance was made by Juan María Gutiérrez in 1852.[1] Since the critic was familiar with only a small portion of the total works, most of his remarks concern the different professions, especially doctors, and types who were satirized by the poet. Textual citations provide a clearer view of what Gutiérrez says. Besides mentioning the lewd or pornographic nature of some of the works, the critic points out some literary precedents for poetry of a satirical nature, but concedes that it is likely that Caviedes acquired much of his satirical wit from adversity and not from other literary figures. One technique which

---

[1] Juan María Gutiérrez, *Escritores coloniales americanos*, ed. Gregorio Weinberg (Buenos Aires, 1957). The study was first published in *El Comercio* of Lima in January, 1852.

is recognized and described by this critic is the use of hyperbole, which is quite common in many poems. Gutiérrez not only comments favorably on some aspects of Caviedes' works, but also censures others; he says:

> Un metro más noble que el romance, el auxilio del consonante que tanto relieve da a la poesía y la ausencia del retruécano, darían a los pensamientos de Caviedes la elevación y la dignidad que al escribirlos tenía en la cabeza. (p. 278)

But he praises him later for not following unswervingly the literary schools of Góngora and Gracián, which the critic seems to consider as being in bad taste. Of the combined works of the poet, familiar to him through a manuscript, the critic says:

> Esta curiosa y olvidada colección es una rara mezcla de desnudeces y de sucios chistes, de juguetes inocentes, de epigramas mordaces, de críticas severas, de quejas amorosas, y de afectos, de un alma contrita, expresados a veces en lenguaje digno del sentimiento que los inspira. (p. 281).

Although the language that Gutiérrez uses here is far from being explicit, one can see that he did have some insight into Caviedes' works and was able to point out at least some of their more obvious features.

The next to write of Caviedes' works, although not entirely in the capacity of literary critic, was Ricardo Palma, first in 1873 and again for his edition of the works in 1899.[2] One can easily see from what he has to say how general ideas about the poet's works became so distorted. Palma says, "Este libro escandalizará oídos susceptibles, sublevará estómagos delicados y no faltará quien lo califique de desvergonzadamente inmoral."[3] These judgments are evidently based on less than three percent of the total works and can only be termed a gross distortion of the true

---

[2] Ricardo Palma, "Prólogo muy preciso", in *Documentos literarios del Perú*, ed. Manuel de Odriozola (Lima, 1873), V, 5-8. See also Palma, "Prólogo", in *Flor de Academias y Diente del Parnaso* (Lima, 1899), p. 335.
[3] Palma, "Prólogo muy preciso", p. 7.

facts. The remainder of what Palma says, in which there is little of real value, involves general platitudes on the satirical nature of some of the works. The same ideas are reiterated again in the prologue to the 1899 edition with no substantial changes in his opinions about Caviedes' poetic production.

In 1894 Menéndez y Pelayo, in his *Antología de poetas hispanoamericanos* (Vol. III, ccx-ccxiii), ventured a few judgments of the poet's works, but primarily cites the previously mentioned study done by Palma.

> Un solo poeta peruano de fines del siglo XVII logró, merced a lo humilde de su condición y al género en que principalmente hubo de ejercitar su travieso ingenio, librarse de la plaga del gongorismo, pero no del conceptismo, o más bien del equivoquismo rastrero y de la afición a retruécanos y juegos de palabras. (p. ccx)

In reply to those who say that the poet is much like Quevedo, this critic states that he should not be confused with the *turbamulta* of Quevedo's imitators, but be considered more akin to the picaresque poets such as Gerardo Lobo and Diego de Torres.

In 1914 the *cuentista* and critic Ventura García Calderón proposed a somewhat different approach to Caviedes' poetry.[4] He sees the poet's importance as being the first to represent and define *la literatura vernal* or *criollismo*, which established a precedent for such writers as Felipe Pardo, Manuel Ascencio Segura, Manuel Atanasio Fuentes, and Ricardo Palma. He also says of the poet, "Es el primer realista, es el único que parece haber mirado bien la pintoresca vida del coloniaje" (p. 330). Besides a brief recounting of Caviedes' ficticious biography, García Calderón dwells primarily on the people whom the poet satirized. One obvious misjudgment by the critic is found in the statement that "Sus temas [de Caviedes], su inspiración, son nacionales" (p. 333). In some of the works this is true, but Caviedes' poetry is certainly not regional in all of its multiple aspects. It would

---

[4] Ventura García Calderón, "La literatura peruana (1535-1914)", *Revue Hispanique*, XXI (1914), 305-391.

seem that the critic has been overly influenced by his desire to stress the poet's *criollismo*.

Four years later Javier Prado continued with remarks in much the same vein as those of García Calderón.[5] He stresses above all that Caviedes was the great precursor of the *criollistas*, but also mentions a few other salient aspects of the poet's works. Though negative in tone, Prado is well aware of the *conceptismos* and *prosaísmos de mal gusto* which remind him of Quevedo's works, although he is quick to say that Caviedes' *criollismo* greatly separates him from the former. Besides a few textual citations used to corroborate observations on Creole elements in some of the works, there is nothing pertinent about any of the facets of the poet's art other than the satirical works.

Although the Peruvian critic and literary historian Luis Alberto Sánchez has written much about Caviedes' life, most of which is equivocal, he says little about the merits or characteristics of the works. In *Los poetas de la colonia y de la revolución* (1921), he says that "Caviedes es el primer revolucionario, y el más ilustre poeta colonial," besides pointing out his importance as the first *criollo* poet of Peru.[6] In addition to recounting the names of numerous people who where satirized by the poet, Sánchez also notes that a later period of Caviedes' writings is more serene and contemplative than that of the satirical period. There is no further attempt, however, to develop these ideas. Sánchez' impressions seem to have changed little in subsequent studies since 1921.[7] The most difficult thing to understand is why he has persisted in rehashing the facts about Caviedes' life, especially his place of birth, when conclusive proof of his Andalusian origin has long since been presented. Unfortunately this problem has been the center of the critic's attention in most of his articles on Caviedes

---

[5] Javier Prado, *El genio de la lengua y de la literatura castellana y sus caracteres en la historia intelectual del Perú* (Lima, 1918), pp. 69-74.

[6] Luis Alberto Sánchez, *Los poetas de la colonia y de la revolución* (Lima, 1947), p. 175. The same remarks on Caviedes were made earlier in 1921 when the work was published in part as *Los poetas de la colonia*.

[7] The same basic ideas are evidenced in *La literatura del Perú* (Buenos Aires, 1939), pp. 60-62 and "Un Villón criollo", *Revista Iberoamericana*, II (April, 1940), 79-86.

with the result that he presents very little in the way of constructive descriptions or evaluations.

José G. Tagle in 1942 also offered some pertinent remarks about Caviedes' stature as a poet, even though much of what he says is colored by false biographical data.[8] He recognizes that Caviedes' poems are not scandalously immoral as Palma and others had seemed to think, but terms them rather "una crítica muy al desnudo de la medicina y los médicos" (p. 27). Most of the descriptions of the poet's works are limited to a few citations from the satires of doctors with an utter disregard for his other contributions.

Although it may be somewhat unusual, one of the most accurate judgments of the poet's works is found in a history of colonial culture in Spanish America by Mariano Picón-Salas.[9] In one of its chapters entitled "El barroco de Indias," Picón-Salas points out some salient features of Caviedes' works, especially as regards epoch style. He says of the poet:

> Juan de Caviedes representa la reacción de lo popular frente a lo amanerado y lo culto... es un Quevedo menor y mucho más lego, menos paralogizado, también, por los símbolos eruditos, en cuyos versos parece prolongarse en América la línea desenfadada y vital de la picaresca. (pp. 124-125)

He compares him to Molière in his manner of making fun of physical pain, in his disillusionment with bad doctors, and his sentimental frustration. As to the poet's baroque qualities, he says:

> Es barroco no tanto en el enrevesamiento de la forma —como ingenio lego ha podido librarse de la pedantería de los catedráticos—, sino en la expresividad y la violencia de su burla, en la crudeza de su grosería, en un como sadismo de lo desagradable. (p. 125)

The writer also points out the prevalent theme of death in the works, and refutes Palma's ideas that the irony and satire of the poet's works are entirely *criollo* in origin.

---

[8] José G. Tagle, *Los culteranos en el Perú* (Lima, 1942), pp. 26-29.
[9] Mariano Picón-Salas, *De la conquista a la independencia* (Mexico, 1944), pp. 124-127.

The Argentine Emilio Carilla, in a study of *gongorismo* in Spanish America and again in a study of Quevedo, offers still more about Caviedes' kinship to the peninsular baroque poets.[10] In the former he points out the "metáforas e hipérboles cultistas" which he believes very reminiscent of Calderón in some works, especially in the "Romances amorosos," but adds that Caviedes' most obvious model was Quevedo. In the second of these studies, he states that he believes Caviedes to be the first satirist of importance in the New World. The remainder of this particular study is devoted to pointing out specific similarities between Quevedo and Caviedes by citing textual evidence. He ends the study by asserting that although the influence of Quevedo's writings on those of Caviedes is clear, it is not so pronounced as to make him nothing more than a vain imitator.

An article in the *Revista Iberoamericana* in 1947 by Luis Fabio Xammar was the first in which a critic tried to present an objective, clearly defined view of the poet and his works;[11] Xammar called the occasion the "nacimiento de una nueva fisonomía de Caviedes" (p. 75). Following a brief, but accurate biographical sketch of the poet, Xammar points out some of the more general characteristics of the works. He quite logically mentions that Caviedes' satire probably belongs to his creative youth and early maturity, while the religious poetry seems to be from his later years. As a specific characteristic of the works, Xammar says that the metaphors used in the satirical poems are "verdaderas *bombas atómicas*," while in addition he notes that many of the people satirized were real and not fictional creations of the poet (p. 82). Textual citations corroborate the critic's cognizance of the use of metaphors and comparisons which involve a good knowledge of gambling terms, especially of card and dice game. A final reference to the religious works, especially to some of the sonnets, describes them as being mystic. Without challenging this statement as equivocal, one would have to entertain a very broad definition

---

[10] Emilio Carilla, *El gongorismo en América* (Buenos Aires, 1946), pp. 97-99; see also *Quevedo, entre dos centenarios* (Tucumán, Argentina, 1949), pp. 222-229.

[11] Luis Fabio Xammar, "La poesía de Juan del Valle Caviedes en el Perú colonial", *Revista Iberoamericana*, XII (1947), 75-91.

of the term in order to apply it properly to Caviedes' works. Even though the article is general in what it covers, Xammar is one of the few who seems to have correct opinions about at least some aspects of Caviedes' poetic art.

The most comprehensive and penetrating study of the poet's works to be published before 1959 was that of Guillermo Lohmann Villena; it appeared in 1948 in the *Revista de Indias*.[12] The initial portions of the article consist of a brief examination of the historical and cultural epoch in which the poet lived and a sketch of his life. In the sections entitled "La obra" and "Lenguaje y estilo de Caviedes", the critic draws particular attention to the balance of Caviedes' poetry between the satirical works on the one hand and the religious on the other. In regards to the poet's language, the critic mentions the existence of some *arcaísmos*, but also points out the tendency toward the use of popular language. Stylistic elements mentioned by Villena include the existence of *retruécanos, juegos de palabras,* the use of hyperbole, metaphors based on card playing terminology, and the evidence of hyperbaton in a large number of works. In addition to these general, but penetrating remarks, the critic points out a few of the parallels between Caviedes and Quevedo, especially in some individual works, but also notes substantial differences between the two. The remainder of the study is devoted to an examination of some of the bibliographical problems associated with the poet's works.

A return to the importance of Caviedes as a *criollista* is found as a primary point of emphasis in Augusto Tamayo Vargas' *Literatura peruana* (1953). This Peruvian critic and literary historian seems cognizant of Caviedes' kinship to certain peninsular writers, but his attitude toward such relationships is entirely negative. He says, "No importa su emparentamiento con Quevedo u otros autores hispanos. Es propia; nuestra".[13] Aside from a few illustrative examples from the satirical and religious works, the only other elements considered briefly are some of the verse forms and

---

[12] Guillermo Lohmann Villena, "Un poeta virreinal del Perú: Juan del Valle Caviedes", *Revista de Indias*, no. 33-34 (1948), 771-794.
[13] Augusto Tamayo Vargas, *Literatura peruana* (Lima, 1953), I, 300.

the most important bibliographical sources, including editions of the works and criticism.

The only book to be published on Caviedes' life and works appeared in 1959.[14] In it Glen L. Kolb studies the satire of the works which he divides into several different categories. These include "Satire of Doctors", "Women: Love, Humor, and Pornographic Satire", "Religious Poetry and Anti-clerical Satire", and "Miscellaneous Verse". The study is primarily oriented toward subject matter and not toward poetic analysis. Nonetheless, it is the most complete of all the studies yet done of Caviedes' works. Although it does include an evaluation and conclusion, there is very little of either to be found. The writer cites the opinions of a few others, especially Emilio Carilla and Lohmann Villena, but offers few evaluative or conclusive statements of his own. Perhaps one of the book's most outstanding attributes is the fact that it includes a basic, although incomplete bibliography of critical articles and references. It might be noted that this study is chiefly an enlargement on the basic ideas presented by Lohmann Villena in his previously cited article, with the principal interest here focused on the element of satire in its various manifestations in the poet's works.

Some idea of Caviedes' importance and place among his literary contemporaries in Spanish America is provided by the comments made by Enrique Anderson Imbert in his literary history of Spanish America, although they are rather brief. He says, "Baste mencionar al más importante de los satíricos de esta época: Juan del Valle Caviedes".[15] The remainder of his remarks are primarily of a descriptive nature, including some observations on the different facets of the poet's artistic development, his similarities to Quevedo, and some of the most commonly used verse forms. His final statement — "Su poesía...es de lo más fresco del Perú colonial" (p. 113) — gives some idea of the importance that this

---

[14] Glen L. Kolb, *Juan del Valle y Caviedes. A Study of the Life, Times and Poetry of a Spanish Colonial Satirist* (New London, Connecticut, 1959).

[15] Enrique Anderson Imbert, *Historia de la literatura hispanoamericana* (Mexico, 1961), I, 112.

noted critic and literary historian attributes to Caviedes' poetic production.

In sum, it has been noted that the criticism of Caviedes' works has taken two general lines of development. One group has predominantly focused its attention on biographical elements with an attempt to relate them to the poet's satirical works. Many of the writers in this same group have insisted on the importance of the *criollo* aspects of the works with an almost complete disregard for any other important features. In many cases an inadequate perspective has resulted in a distorted picture of the overall aspects of the poet's works. The other group, composed primarily of the more recent critics, has tried to give some idea of the different facets of the poet's art as well as a description of some of the basic elements of which it consists. Nonetheless, there is no work which attempts a comprehensive study of the poet's entire production.

PART II
ANALYSIS OF POETIC WORKS

ANALYSIS OF POETIC WORKS

A thorough examination of the two hundred sixty-eight poems, which comprise Caviedes' total known contribution, shows that they can be divided into four major divisions with some subdivisions. Three of these divisions seem to coincide with what might be different periods of development in the poet's art. Since the vast majority of Caviedes' poems cannot be dated or placed in any chronological order, the basis for division has been made in part on aspects of style, technique, subject matter, and themes. The subsequent analysis of the poet's works will provide sufficient evidence for assuming that this type of grouping of the works is both feasible and logical.

The first group which will be considered is made up of works of an amorous nature. These thirty-five poems have generally been overshadowed in importance by the satirical works. They include comments on the nature and essence of love as well as poems addressed to various women whose beauty as well as disdain inspired the poet to write about them.

The largest of these groups contains one hundred thirty-two poems which have social satire as a common characteristic. Fifty of these are directly concerned with medical quackery, physicians, and the general field of medicine. Fifty-two others satirize different professionals such as tailors, clergymen, poets, and actors. Also included in this group are satires of drunkards, Negroes, mulattoes, and people with physical deformities, while women are also the brunt of the poet's virulent attacks. Thirty poems treat *alcahuetas,* prostitutes, *feas,* doctor's wives, and others. Many of the poems of a lewd or pornographic nature are found in this group.

The third major division is made up of thirty-two poems of a religious nature. They deal principally with different phases of Catholicism and have as their subjects God, Jesus Christ, Mary, and some saints. Included in this group is a large number of lyric poems in which the narrator confesses his sinful actions and asks God for his mercy.

The fourth and final division of poems contains those on miscellaneous subjects. For the most part they treat contemporary and classical subjects with others being of a more meditative nature. The latter include observations on riches, poverty, life, and especially on death. The remainder of this division is made up of what might be called occasional verse. Twenty-eight of these are *agudas* and *epigramas* which are short (four or five verses) poems on a variety of subjects with usually only one thought being evoked. They are, in a sense, short witticisms or sayings. One other poem of this group worthy of special note at this point is the "Carta que escribió el autor a la monja de México habiéndose ésta enviado a pedir algunas obras de sus versos, siendo ella en esto y en todo el mayor ingenio de estos siglos", which was written to Sor Juana Inés de la Cruz.

Ten poems found in some of the manuscripts containing Caviedes' works are not included in this study, since they are of doubtful paternity. The first of these, "Lamentaciones sobre la vida en pecado", is most certainly not by Caviedes.[1] It was in fact written by Juan Martínez de Cuéllar, a Spaniard, and was published as a part of his work, *El desengaño del hombre en el tribunal de la fortuna y casa de descontentos* (1663). The poem was either copied by Caviedes or later added to the manuscripts of his poetry by some copyist. The other nine poems which have been excluded from this study are found in varying versions in the *Actas* of the *Tertulia* of the Marqués Castell dos Rius who was viceroy of Peru and patron of the arts.[2] He gathered about him many erudite nobles who attended the *Tertulia* during 1709

---

[1] Emilio Carilla, "Restituciones a la lírica española", RFH, VIII (1946), 148-150.

[2] *Flor de Academias y Diente del Parnaso*, ed. Ricardo Palma (Lima, 1899). The sessions of the *Tertulia* met on Mondays from September 23, 1709, to March 24, 1710.

and 1710. Pedro de Peralta Barnuevo, the author of *Lima fundada*, was one of those who regularly participated in the sessions. It is difficult to tell whether the poems in question were originally written by Caviedes and then plagarized by the *contertulianos* or vice versa, since none of the manuscripts is an autograph and it is impossible to affix a precise date to the existing copies, thus showing them to antedate the sessions of the *Tertulia*. A future stylistic study of these works may definitively prove whether they do or do not belong to Caviedes. They include the "Romance en que forzosamente acaban sus versos con letras que por sí solas hablan y muchas veces empiezan" (MSS. Yale-A, Duke, Lima-A, Lima-B, and Molíns), "Lamentos de una pobre mujer y consuelos de un pobre marido, por la distinta naturaleza de sus consortes" (MSS. Yale-A, Duke, Madrid, Lima-B and Molíns), "Coplas que acaban con puntos y letras por sí solas" (MSS. Yale-A, Lima-A, Lima-B, and Molíns), "Romance a lo divino con ecos dobles al fin de cada verso" (MSS. Yale-A, Duke, Lima-A, Lima-B, and Molíns), "Otro al mismo asumpto" (MSS. Yale-A, Duke, Lima-A, and Molíns), "A un sordo" (MSS. Yale-A, Duke, Madrid, Lima-B, and Molíns), "Goza del Marquez de Castell dos Rius" (MS. Duke), "¿Cuál sea mejor para mujer propia, la hermosa boba o la fea discreta?" (MSS. Yale-A, Duke, Madrid, Lima-B, and Molíns), and "Manda a uno que elija de tres cosas la que le parece mejor, a saber: título, coche o mujer y da la razón que tiene para elegir coche o no título ni mujer" (MSS. Yale-A, Lima-B, and Molíns).

The actual methods to be applied in the analysis of each poem are in part a combination of techniques adapted primarily from two basic sources, Wolfgang Kayser's *Interpretación y análisis de la obra literaria* (2nd. ed., 1958) and Monroe C. Beardsley's *Aesthetics* (1958).[3] The first of these is of a more practical

---

[3] Among other works of considerable value in questions of literary theory and criticism, one may find the following: Cleanth Brooks and Robert Penn Warren, *Understanding Poetry;* Kenneth Burke, *The Philosophy of Literary Form; The Poem Itself,* ed. Stanley Burnshaw *et al.;* Thomas Clark Pollock, *The Nature of Literature;* Ivor Armstrong Richards, *Practical Criticism;* René Wellek and Austin Warren, *Theory of Literature;* William Kurtz Wimsatt, Jr., *The Verbal Icon.* See the "List of Works Consulted"

nature, since it develops a variety of techniques which can be utilized in the analysis of a literary work. Not only are the various possible techniques discussed, but they are also applied to the works in a display of the practicality of the methodology which the author suggests. The ideas which the book contains are not, of course, the pure invention of the author, but represent an accumulation of ideas from various sources as the extensive bibliography contained in the work well indicates. Although Beardsley's *Aesthetics* does not offer so practical an approach to literary analysis, it is of particular value in some aspects of poetic analysis. In this study it has been consulted primarily as a source for different theories of poetic analysis and explication, as well as evaluation. His chapters on "The Literary Work", "Form in Literature", and "Literature and Knowledge" have been found extremely valuable not only for the ideas espoused by the writer, but also for the interesting "Notes and Inquiries" at the end of each chapter in which different theories of explication and techniques of analysis are discussed and criticized. It should be understood, however, that even though these two works contain many of the main precepts incorporated into the methodology of this analysis, they are not necessarily the exclusive ideas of either of these writers, but represent an accumulation of ideas from innumerable sources.

Since the literary work, in this case poetry, contains deep levels of meaning that are only hinted at through connotation and suggestion, a literary discourse has a kind of semantical thickness or depth when compared with mathematical and technical discourse. As Monroe C. Beardsley in his *Aesthetics* asserts, "There are meanings that we do not see unaided, but acknowledge to be present as soon as they are pointed out to us. To point out the meaning in a poem is to *explicate* the poem" (p. 129). Thus, it is evident that in order to arrive at an understanding of the meaning of a poem, one must first discover what the component parts of the work are as well as the techniques utilized in its creation. The greatest danger in this kind of

---

at the end of this study for more complete information on each of these works.

analysis is that the critic is often prone to consider the technical aspects in such a manner as to disregard completely the fact that they are only the tools with which the poet has constructed his literary world of the work. Cleanth Brooks and Robert Penn Warren in their book, *Understanding Poetry* (New York, 1960), warn of this pitfall.

> We have seen then, that a poem is not to be thought of as merely a bundle of things which are "poetic" in themselves. Nor is it to be thought of, as the "message hunters" would seem to have it, as a kind of box, decorated or not, in which a "truth" or a "fine sentiment" is hidden.
> Certainly it is not to be thought of as a group of *mechanically* combined elements—meter, rhyme, figurative language, idea and so on—put together to make a wall. The relationship among the elements in a poem is what is all important; it is not a mechanical relationship but one which is far more intimate and fundamental (p. 16).

It is hoped, therefore, that the analysis of the mechanical aspects of Caviedes' poertry can be projected toward an understanding of the individual poems as well as the combined poetic worlds created by the writer.

Apart from the analysis of the "world of the work",[4] some valuable information can be obtained from sources outside this fictional world. In such cases these elements serve to elucidate those factors which are not self-explained through an explication of the text itself. One example of the need for elucidation from exterior sources is seen in the matter of the physicians whom Caviedes satirizes. It is essential to know that the majority of them are not purely fictional creations of the poet's mind, but actually existed in seventeenth century Peru.

---

[4] Monroe C. Beardsley, *Aesthetics* (New York, 1958), p. 115. Beardsley defines the literary work as a "set of human actions, imagined or conceived. Actions involve actors and settings; this totality of persons, places, and things I shall call the world of the work". The definition is applicable, of course, to all the genres.

In order to arrive at some concept of what the poetic art of Caviedes consists, it is necessary to look for certain elements within each poem. The basic elements which will be considered in this analysis of his art are form, including structure and technique, which make up style, and content.

Within the realm of form one must consider the structural elements of each poem. This involves ascertaining the type of verse form as well as the kinds of rhythms used. Another structural element is the strophe form together with any rhyme scheme which the poem might have. The point of view of the narrator or speaker is another factor to be considered at the same time. The narrator either knows what is occurring in the actor's mind or he doesn't and he can either observe his external actions or he cannot. Beardsley defines point of view as the "spatial perspective from which the speaker observes the events he describes" (pp. 247-248). At times the literary work may be addressed to a special person or audience. When this is true, one might say that the work has an implicit receiver. If there is an implicit receiver, it is sometimes possible to detect the speaker's attitude toward the receiver. This is often called the tone of the work, although tone can be used in a more general sense.

Under the broad concept of style, it would seem proper and worthwhile to point out those salient features of epoch style common to other contemporary works of the period. Since the entirety of Caviedes' poetic production is limited to the second half of the seventeenth century, the poet was quite logically influenced most, although not exclusively, by the baroque movement which was prevalent in the Peninsula. One has only to examine the works of such contemporaries of Caviedes as Sor Juana Inés de la Cruz and Carlos de Sigüenza y Góngora in Mexico to see that its far-reaching influence was felt throughout the Hispanic World during that century. Therefore, it is of some value to see exactly what stylistic and conceptual features of Caviedes' art are in accord with the general characteristics of the Baroque.[5]

---

[5] René Wellek, "The Concept of Baroque in Literary Scholarship", *Journal of Aesthetics and Art Criticism*, V (1946), 77-109. This work offers a short concise summary of the concept of the Baroque and of literary char-

Other features of style which can be considered are the rhetorical features or figurative language of the poems. They have little intrinsic value in themselves, but when they are considered as a part of the entire poem and the poet's art, they can be appreciated as a whole. Kayser in his *Interpretación y análisis* discusses and defines a variety of these rhetorical features. [6] He also points out that these figures should not be taken as the only stylistic features of a work, since it is a combination of these and other features coupled with the recurrence of secondary meaning which really constitute the style of a writer. Other elements of style considered in the poems are those of lexical peculiarities and syntactical features such as phraseology and sentence structure.

Under the division of content several subjects are treated. The first of these is subject matter. Beardsley suggests the following as a definition of subject matter:

> In every literary work there is, besides the speaker, a set of objects or events that confront him, which he may call his *situation*. In this broad sense, the situation is the *subject* of the work—what is found, or met with, what happens or appears, in it. It is, in one sense, what the work is about (p. 240).

In some cases the situation is a chain of events. In these cases the work is a narrative and the speaker may be thought of as a narrator. In a few of Caviedes' poems such narrative elements do appear.

One usually asks if there is not some general idea that connects the variety of general references to the subject of a work.

---

acteristics generally found in works influenced by this epoch style; of course there are numerous other works on the subject, v. "List of Works Consulted."

[6] Wolfgang Kayser, *Interpretación y análisis de la obra literaria*, trans. M. D. Mouton and V. G. Yebra (Madrid, 1958), pp. 175-203. Kayser's list of rhetorical figures includes paronomasia, allusion, periphrasis, irony, hyperbole, synecdoche and metonymy, metaphor, synesthesia, imagery, catachresis, oxymoron, antithesis, enumeration, parallelism, anaphora, chiasmus, and zeugma. See also, *Dictionary of World Literature*, ed. Joseph T. Shipley (Patterson, New Jersey, 1960).

If some concept does seem to relate these references, then they may be considered to be the theme. In a short definition Beardsley suggests that a theme is something named by an abstract noun or phrase in contrast to the subject which is referred to by a concrete noun or nominative construction (p. 403). He also adds that if in some cases it can be said that there is a "general statement that the work may be said to afford, or to contain, which makes some observation or reflection about life or art, man or reality, then this doctrine or ideological content may be called the thesis of the poem" (p. 403). Although not every poem will have a thesis, it will usually have some sort of theme or themes. Both theme and thesis in a literary work can be determined by an interpretation of the work.

The characters which appear at times in the world of the work also form a part of the content. As in the case of Caviedes' poetry, it has been mentioned that there are often recurring appearances by certain characters. When possible an effort has been made to identify these real people. Their identification is of no great importance to an explication of the literary world of the work, but for matters of elucidation they do provide a solid link between the fictitious world and the world of reality.

Chapter IV

FORMS OF AMOROUS POETRY [1]

The thirty-five poems which will be considered in this first part of the analysis of Caviedes' works are those which deal with amorous themes and subject matter. The basic nucleus of the group consists of sixteen "Romances amorosos" which do not have individual titles, but are numbered respectively "I" through "XVI". [2] The entire group does not represent especially the most important period of Caviedes' development as a poet, but does seem to be the initial stage of his art. As will be noted in subsequent chapters, Caviedes' style and technique are considerably more developed in his other types of poetry than they are in these particular works. Also, the style, situations, and themes in these poems seem more typical of transitional works between the Renaissance and Baroque than they do of any one specific

---

[1] Form in this and subsequent chapters refers not to just the limited concept of form as structure, but to the more encompassing concept of the combined features of the poetic work with the exception of content. Since content and form cannot be separated, the introductory portions of each chapter and division will deal specifically with general features of content; the remainder of the unit will be devoted to a consideration of the various aspects of form, especially style, structure, and techniques. For a more detailed analysis of the concept of form, see Monroe C. Beardsley, *Aesthetics* (New York, 1958), pp. 165-168.

[2] *Obras de Don Juan del Valle y Caviedes*, ed. Rubén Vargas Ugarte (Lima, 1947), pp. 61-73. The following textual citations in this and subsequent chapters are from this edition, hereafter cited as *Obras*, unless otherwise stated; in the text, however, only page numbers will be given for this edition.

epoch style. The features of *conceptismo* and *culteranismo*, which are evident in the poetry of social satire and religious themes, are without a doubt more representative of later periods of the poet's artistic development.

Insofar as Caviedes' general ideas on love are concerned, it may be said that, as seen in these works, they are for the most part centered around ideal love. It could not be wholly described as Platonic, but does seem to share many similar features. In the sonnet, "Da el autor catorce definiciones al amor," one gets a succinct but figurative summary of what the poet believed love to be.

> Amor es nombre sin deidad segura,
> un agente del ser de cuantos nacen,
> un abreviar la vida a los que yacen,
> un oculto querer a otra criatura,
> una fantasma, asombro de hermosura,
> una falsa opinión que al mundo esparcen,
> un destino de errar en cuanto hacen,
> un delirio que al gusto hace cordura.
> Fuego es de pedernal si está encubierto,
> aires es si a todos baña sin ser visto,
> agua es, por ser vicio de la espuma,
> una verdad, mentira de lo cierto,
> un traidor que, adulando, está bien quisto
> él es enigma y laberinto en suma.
> *(MS. Madrid, 294r-294v)*

A variety of situations is presented in these thirty-five poems, although the majority of them are quite similar in many aspects. Approximately two-thirds of the group present a man's amorous lament to a woman whom he loves, but his beloved disdains and rejects each and every entreaty that he makes. In two different poems the situation involves a *pobre pastor* who is lamenting his misfortune in love (62-63 and 67-68). A mythological situation is presented in the fable of Daphne and Apollo in which the former is turned into a laurel tree to escape the latter's pursuit (64-65). In other situations one sees a *dama* going for a walk in the *prado* on a May day (66), a beautiful woman taking a bath in the presence of Venus and Adonis (109), and a *ruiseñor* that is singing a sad lament (MS. Yale-B, 101v-102r).

The characters who appear in these poems are not real people, as they are in others of Caviedes' works. Besides a large number of unidentified ladies, the poet addresses or mentions Lisi (61), Filis (63), Lisarda (64), Catalina (65), Lucila (66), Lucinda (68), Marcia (69), Amarinda (73), Tomiris (73), Menga (78), Clisi (108), Anarda (108 and 109), and Belisa (MS. Madrid, 248r-249r). Mythological characters include Daphne (77), Apollo (64), Venus (207), and Adonis (109). Besides Aurelio (67) and another unnamed *pastor* (62), a *ruiseñor* (MS. Yale-B, 101v-102r) and some *tórtolas* are also central although not human characters in two other poems (70).

A brief consideration of the point of view in these works gives some insight into the general tone, since in a strict sense tone can be considered as the narrator's attitude toward the person to whom he addresses himself. The major portion of these poems are lyric in nature and have the narrator addressing a lady in the second person singular. The only variations are found in a small number of poems which are narrated completely in the third person, both singular and plural, and are primarily of an informative nature. In the former the tone of the works is quite intimate, since the *yo* of each poem is addressed specifically to a particular woman, as is the case in the following quotation in which the *yo* addresses Daphne:

> Atiende, ingrata Dafne,
> mis quejas, si escucharlas
> te merecen mis penas,
> siquiera por ser tú quien me las causas.
> Bien sé que son al viento
> decirlas a una ingrata;
> pero yo las publico
> para que sepas solo a quien agravias. (77)

In most cases, however, the *yo* is separated from the addressee either by the absence or the disdain of the latter. Insofar as the tone of the subject matter is concerned, one could say that it is both amorous and plaintive. This is generally true, since in most cases the narrator is lamenting his misfortune in love or his having been disdained by a lady.

As might be expected, the most commonly encountered theme in this group of poems is love, which in many of the works is unrequited or unfortunate love (56-58, 61-62, 62-63, 63-64, 65-66, and 73-76). Disdain, usually of a suitor's advances, is another common theme (66, 67-68, 68, 70-71, and 71-72). Feminine beauty is the theme of a small number of poems (68-69, 73-77, 78-79, 109; MS. Madrid, 247r-248r, 248r-249r; and MS. Yale-B, 101v-102r).

The form which most predominates in this group of poems is the *romance*. Eight different combinations of assonance are used in the twenty *romances*, although those of "i-a" and "e-a" appear with greatest frequency. The octosyllabic verses used in them are of three principal classes. Trochaic octosyllables (accents on three and seven) and mixed octosyllables (accents on two and seven) predominate, while one does find an occasional dactylic octosyllabic verse (accents on one and seven). The second most used form is the sonnet of which five are quite characteristic of Caviedes and have a rhyme scheme of ABBA:ABBA in the quatrains and CDC:DCD in the tercets. This rhyme scheme does not represent an innovation on the part of the poet, since it was the most commonly used rhyme in the seventeenth century in Spain, especially so in the sonnets of Calderón, Villamediana, and Quevedo.[3] One sonnet, of which only three appear in Caviedes' works, has a rhyme scheme of ABBA:ABBA in the quatrains, but CDE:CDE in the two tercets. The hendecasyllabic verses in the sonnets are almost equally divided among heroic (accents on two and six), melodic (accents on three and six), and Sapphic (accents on four and six or eight), while an occasional verse is an *endecasílabo enfático* (accents on one and six). Two poems are *décimas espinelas*. All have the abba:ac:cddc rhyme common to this class of *décima*. Two other poems are *coplas de pie quebrado*. Their individual stanzas are of three octosyllabic verses and one final tetrasyllabic verse. The only forms which are found in this group of poems and which do not commonly appear in Caviedes' other works are a *glosa* and three *endechas reales*. The stanzas of the former consist of octosyllabic verses with an initial *redondilla*

---

[3] Tomás Navarro Tomás, *Métrica española* (Syracuse, 1956), p. 234.

followed by four *décimas espinelas* in which the final verse of each corresponds respectively to one of the consecutive verses of the initial *redondilla*. The *endechas reales* have stanzas of four verses with different combinations of assonance. They consist of three initial heptasyllabic and a final hendecasyllabic verse. By their very nature they are usually employed in amorous laments, as is the case in these works.

Internal structure is of particular interest in four different poems (62-63, 64-65, 66-67, and 67-68). In each of these works, the poet begins by presenting a scene or situation in which the character is introduced. The general effect is somewhat drama-like, since after setting the scene, the character then begins a plaintive monologue. In the following exerpt from one of these poems, one sees how the scene is set through a third person descriptive narration in the introduction and then continues with a monologue by Apollo addressed to Daphne:

> En un laurel convertida
> vió Apolo a su Dafne amada
> ¿quién pensara que en lo verde
> murieran sus esperanzas?
> Abrazado con el tronco
> y cubierto con las ramas,
> pegó la boca a los nudos
> y a la corteza la cara.
> Con mil almas le decía
> a la que sin ella estaba:
> No para mí, para tí,
> Dafne, ha sido la mudanza;
> pues tanto vale el ser tronco
> como ser ninfa tirana... (64)

This particular structural development is peculiar only to this one group of poems and is not found in any of the other facets of Caviedes' production.

In contrast to the other obvious baroque features of epoch style to be found in subsequent groups of poems which will be considered, the works presently under consideration present few ostensible elements of *conceptismo* and *culteranismo*. The bucolic nature of some of the poems together with the amorous laments and weeping seem more characteristic of the Renaissance than they do of baroque poetry; however, the use of the traditional *romance* would not seem in keeping with the predominantly Italianate forms of that epoch. In the following quotation from a *romance*, the bucolic nature of some of the situations is quite evident:

> En el regazo de un olmo,
> verde gigante del prado,
> estaba un triste pastor,
> pensativo y sollozando.
> Con la mano en la mejilla
> y el pañuelo en la otra mano,
> así decía a las flores
> las lágrimas enjugando... (62-63)

It would seem most logical and reasonable to assert that these particular works present transitional characteristics that are neither completely renaissance in their multiple aspects nor baroque. It is not particularly surprising, however, since the early works of both Góngora and Quevedo have similar aspects which have been largely overshadowed by the *culteranismo* of the first and the *conceptismo* of the second in their later periods of artistic development.

The majority of the metaphors used in these poems refer primarily to women. They are called "bella homicida" (62), "ausente dueño mío" (71), "hermoso dueño mío" (MS. Madrid, 291r), "Ingrato Dueño esquivo" (56), and "dueño hermoso" (MS. Madrid, 290v-292r). References to Venus as the "Hija del mar inconstante" (207) and to Cupid as "el ciego Dios" (47) are easily understood from even a slight knowledge of their mythological histories. The only other metaphors of note are the references to women's eyes. They are called "Alcaldes de Corte" (MS. Madrid, 248r), "divinos soles" (MS. Madrid, 248v), and "dos luceros" (MS. Madrid, 248r). As can be noted from this partial listing of the metaphors used, they show little ingenuity and the lack of them is in direct contrast to other portions of the poet's works.

Visual imagery predominates in practically all of these poems. In keeping with many of the rustic and pastoral situations which are often presented, the imagery reflects this bucolic nature. In some poems this involves bright and colorful imagery, as in the following quotation:

> Un arroyo fugitivo
> de la cárcel del Diciembre,
> cadenas de cristal rompe
> y lima grillos de nieve.
> ....
> En perlas paga a las flores
> el censo oriental que debe... (68-69)

One sees the same features in the following images: "verde margen / de un cristalino arroyuelo" (67), "el cristal de una fuente" (109), "Roca de plata" (109), and "condensada pella de nieve" (109). Imagery of garden flora is also found, as in the "Romance amoroso VIII" (66-67) in which one sees "el sol," "el prado," "jazmín," "rosas," "fuentes," and "los cristales," while in others the poet speaks of "azucenas," "claveles," and "margaritas" (MS. Madrid, 248v-249v). In all of these examples one sees reflected the bucolic and rustic nature of many of these works.

One auditory image is worthy of specific mention. In it the poet speaks of the sound of water flowing when he says, "El ruido de los cristales / estaba escuchando atento" (67). In yet another poem, one finds an example of synesthesia in which there is a concurrent appeal to both the senses of sight and sound, as one sees in the following:

> la discreción viene a ser
> una hermosura compuesta
> de voces que los oídos
> la ven con ojos de idea... (73)

The most commonly employed rhetorical figure in this group of poems is alliteration. In some cases there seems to be an attempt to reinforce meaning with certain sound patterns. In the verses to follow, one sees how the letter "s", especially initial "s", is repeated in order to remind one of the sound of crying or sobbing: "Mucho más que no la queja / sentir sabe el sufrimiento" (62). In another case the explosive force of initial "p" seems to add emphasis and authority to the command which the narrator gives:

> No tengas piedad de mí
> pues yo no pienso pedirla,
> que el que piedades no busca
> se contenta con tus iras. (65)

Alliteration in the verses to follow is found in the repetition of initial "m" along with the nasal "n". It is not clear whether the use of the technique here adds meaning, but it certainly does emphasize and call attention to what is being said.

> A verte yo y no mirarme
> para mi muerte me citas,
> que ya veo el que me matas
> y el que me muero no miras.
> ....
> Eres tirana sin ver,
> pues sin más ver solicitas
> que muera de no mirado
> el que matas de bien vista. (68)

The use of parallel constructions which is so typical of other facets of Caviedes' poetic production is not in any great evidence in these works. In the previously cited sonnet, "Da el autor catorce definiciones al amor," there is parallelism of dominant elements in a portion of the verses. The various definitions of love are placed in an initial position in the verses to give added emphasis, as one sees in the following: "un agente del ser," "un abreviar la vida," "un oculto querer," "una fantasma," "una falsa opinión," "un destino de errar," and "un delirio" (94-95).

Apostrophe is also used by the poet in some of these works. In three individual poems the *yo* addresses seemingly inanimate objects as though they were alive and could understand or even reply in return. In the first of these the *yo* addresses his *penas* and says:

> Penas, sed más rigurosas
> para alivio del que os pasa,
> que el cuchillo que más corta
> menos aflige al que mata. (61)

In the case of a *pastor* who is lamenting his unfortunate love for Filis, he addresses the flowers which are about him in a sylvan setting:

> Flores, si sabéis de amor
> sentid mi desprecio, en tanto
> que con el lloro que vierto
> vuestro tronco riego en pago. (63)

In the following stanzas the use of apostrophe results in a personification of the inanimate objects addressed, as one sees in the following example in which the *yo* asks if the fountains can see his weeping or if the rocks can hear his laments:

> Fuentes, que veis mi llanto,
> para lágrimas tiernas
> prestadme vuestras aguas,
> pagaré en ríos cristalinas hebras.
> Rocas, si las paredes
> tienen para oír quejas,
> también tendrán los riscos
> oídos que prestar a mis ternezas.
> *(MS. Madrid, 290v)*

A single case of oxymoron is found in the "Romance amoroso I." In it one finds what seems to be a contradiction in the fact that voices should talk with silence: "¡Oh! ¡quien hallara unas voces / que hablasen con el silencio!" (62). This technique is found, however, in some of the other groups of poems to be considered later.

Only one example of internal rhyme is found in the entire group of poems and the technique is somewhat questionable even in this one, since the rhyme seems more casual than intentional. The poet says, "no es mía, que si lo fuera / mas que se perdiera en vos" (48). The two words, *fuera* and *perdiera,* are separated by several lexical elements with the second of the two words serving as a kind of delayed echo of the first.

Insofar as lexicon and syntax are concerned, there is little that need be commented upon. No single lexical element stands out except for the large number of words which are related to or are a part of the pastoral descriptions. A few anthroponyms from mythological sources are evident. "Dafne" (64), "Apolo" (64), "Febo" (69), "Icaro" (58), "Venus" (207), "Adonis" (109), "Cupido" (181), and "Argos" (MS. Madrid, 247r-248r), are among those mentioned most in these poems. No Americanisms nor Latinisms are evident in the general vocabulary. There are few syntactical deviations such as hyperbaton, nor are any other syntactical complexities to be noted. Neither are there any general stylistic features which stand out because of the rarity of their usage or their excessiveness. In the vast majority of the poems, it would seem that lyric expression in a clear, concise language is emphasized and developed much more than are any technical aspects of individual style.

In résumé it may be said that these poems make up what was probably an initial period of the poet's creativity. The amorous themes and subject matter are often presented in bucolic and rustic situations, with the emphasis being placed on the pitiable state of someone who is dying of love and wishes everyone to know of his plight.

Verse forms are primarily traditional with the *romance* predominating over Italianate forms. The single *glosa* and the *endechas reales* are the only strophes which appear only infrequently in other portions of the poet's works.

Features of epoch style are few, but the combination of themes and situations in traditional forms leads one to believe that the works represent a transitional stage of development which was influenced by the currents of both the Renaissance and the Baroque.

Aside from basic metaphors and imagery, the only techniques which stand out are the use of alliteration and personification. A few isolated cases of parallelism, internal rhyme, oxymoron, and synesthesia are also to be found, but are not of major consequence.

No salient lexical elements are to be noted, except for a few classical allusions to mythological characters and words closely related to bucolic situations. The syntax of the works is clear and concise and presents no features which might stand out as individual traits of the poet's style.

Although these poems do not necessarily represent the most important facet of Caviedes' works, they are perhaps the most lyric. The poet's expression of his most intimate sentiments is possibly more evident in these works of an amorous nature than they are in many of the other poems. Nonetheless, they do not seem to show the same level of artistic development that one finds in either the satirical or religious poetry.

Chapter V

FORMS OF POETRY OF SOCIAL SATIRE

A. Medical Satire

Within the broad division of poetry of social satire, there are fifty poems by Caviedes which deal explicitly with doctors and medical quackery. They form the nucleus of the satirical *Diente del Parnaso,* which was the only titled book produced by the poet. Too, they have been the poems most cited by literary critics and historians when mentioning Caviedes' poetic production. Perhaps they have overshadowed the other three-fifths of the poems because of their vehemence in attacking the various members of Lima's medical profession as well as medical practices of the epoch.

Caviedes was well aware of the fact that he was not an innovator in satires and general verbal attacks on medical men. In the "Romance jocoserio o a saltos al asunto que el dirá, si lo preguntasen los ojos que quisieren leerlo" (312-322), the poet cites the attacks made against doctors by such persons as Seneca, Socrates, Diogenes, Aristotle, Pithagoras, Democritus, Cicero, Empedocles, Isaiah, Tertullian, Juvenal, Martial, Pliny, St. Augustine, Alfonso X el Sabio, Plutarch, Erasmus, and Philip IV of Spain. Among literary figures of his own century he mentions Quevedo, Villamediana, Cervantes, Calderón, Luis Vélez, and Moreto. By supporting himself with the opinions of all these, Caviedes thus justifies the cause for such invectives, while at the same time he presents a kind of historical background for these poems.

In his "Prólogo" to the *Diente del Parnaso,* Caviedes gives something of a statement of purpose which he addresses to the reader of the work:

> Más médico es mi tratado
> que ellos, pues si bien se mira,
> divierte que es un remedio
> que cura de hipocondría;
> pues para los accidentes
> que son de melancolía,
> no hay nada que los alivie
> como un récipe de risa.
> Ríete de tí el primero,
> pues con la fé más sencilla
> piensas que el médico entiende
> el mal que le comunicas.
> Ríete de ellos después,
> que su brutal avaricia
> venden por ciencia, sin alma,
> tan a costa de las vidas.
> Ríete de todo, puesto
> que aunque de todo te rías
> tienes razón.—Dios te guarde,
> sin médicos ni boticas. (217)

From what is said here, one can readily assume that Caviedes' invectives against doctors are primarily intended to make people laugh, and it may be added that the reader of these satirical works can hardly help but agree that the poet achieves his purpose. This should not, however, mislead anyone into thinking that Caviedes was insincero in his purpose. In another poem he says:

> No son caprichos mis versos,
> como los médicos piensan
> y publican que es manía
> de agudo, imperioso tema. (315)

And he adds at the end of the same poem:

> En burlas y veras trata
> de los médicos mi vena;
> pero en mi sangre no traten
> ni de burlas ni de veras. (322)

Caviedes' strong dislike for doctors was very real and everpresent and it stimulated his wit enough to write the major portion of the poems contained in the *Diente del Parnaso*.

It has been suggested by one of Caviedes' earlier biographers that the poet's beginning to assail doctors in verse was coincidental with his recovery from a serious illness during which he suffered from the medical ineptness of the doctors who attended him.[1] Whether or not this is true is of little or no importance, since the works exist whatever the stimulus, and they can be appreciated as entities in themselves rather than having to rely on sociological or exterior factors from the poet's biography to make them interesting.

This group of poems shows Caviedes to be primarily a popular and traditional poet. The subject matter is not limited to an upper elite of readers, but would seem to appeal to the popular element of society as well. With this observation is also coupled the fact that of the fifty poems contained in the group, thirty-nine are written in popular and traditional forms. There are only four sonnets and seven *décimas espinelas*. Only one of the sonnets actually forms a part of the *Diente del Parnaso*, while the others are from his miscellaneous verse. All of them have the same rhyme scheme of ABBA:ABBA in the two quatrains and CDC: DCD in the two tercets. Twenty-nine of the poems are *romances* of varied combinations of assonance. In a few short poems called *epigramas* and *agudas*, one finds *redondillas* and *quintillas*, but their small number is of little significance alongside the larger quantity of *romances*. One *letrilla*, a form usually employed in satire, is also found in this group of poems (292-294). It, too, has a popular subject; and in it Caviedes chides his compatriots' lack of awareness of the doctors' malpractices, when he says that the people fear earthquakes more than they do doctors. The *letrilla* is composed of stanzas of ten octosyllabic verses and has the same *estribillo* repeated as a refrain at the end of each of the stanzas.

These observations on verse and strophe can be synthesized

---

[1] Juan María Gutiérrez, "Don Juan Caviedes, fragmento de unos estudios sobre la literatura poética del Perú", in *Documentos literarios del Perú*, ed. Manuel de Odriozola (Lima, 1873), V, 10.

by saying that they present no radical innovations. The *romance,* utilized by Caviedes in sixty percent of the works, was probably chosen by the poet because of the popular nature of his subject matter. The Italianate form had less appeal for the poet as can be seen by the fact that it is found only in the four sonnets.

Caviedes, as the narrator, does not usually enter into the individual poems as one of their characters, but does maintain an intimate relationship with the world of the work. In most of the poems the narrator directly addresses the main character(s) of the poem, thus putting himself in personal contact with them. This can be seen in the initial verses of the following quotation:

> Con imprudentes arrojos
> partos no pronostiquéis,
> que en preñados entendéis
> teniendo tantos anteojos. (271)

One exception to this general technique is the "Carta que escribió el autor al Dr. Herrera, el tuerto, a quien llevó de esta ciudad a la de Quito el presidente y le hizo protomédico y catedrático de prima del rastro de la medicina" (300-303). In it the poet enters the world of the work as an active participant and addresses Dr. Herrera:

> Herrera, la enhorabuena
> en esta os doy del oficio
> que estáis ejerciendo de
> protoverdugo de Quito.
> ... ...
> De tal parte, día tantos
> de tal mes; con esto evito
> vuestras curas que no saben
> cómo, cuándo y porqué han sido. (300-303)

One other poem offers a different technique, since the author takes an active role as a character in the poem, while at the same time serving as the narrator within the world of the work. In the poem "Causa" Caviedes is the "Juez pesquisidor de los errores médicos, en Lima" and he in turn narrates the series of events of a petition placed before him (288-292).

Only two poems have radically different types of narrators. In the "Respuesta de la Muerte" (225-226), Death, as a personified character, appears to address Dr. don Terciana, who is about to die. In the poem entitled "Parecer que da de esta obra la anatomía del Hospital de San Andrés" (217-222), the hospital, personified, is the narrator and main character of the poem. These, however, are exceptions to the general technique utilized. In general the narrator is omniscient and is aware of all that is going on within the realm of the world of the work.

In practically every poem there is a specific person (or persons) to whom the narrator addresses himself. Usually doctors are the ones under personal attack by the poet. In the "Loa en aplauso de el Dr. Francisco Machuca por haver curado a una prima del autor y averla muerto como todos los que cura" (259-262), one sees that the narrator is directing himself quite pointedly at Dr. Machuca and at the same time makes cutting remarks about ugly women.

> Verdugo atroz, inhumano,
> cuya bárbara fiereza
> de idiota ignorancia es tanta
> que no perdona bellezas;
> ¿por qué, verdugo en latín,
> no te das a curar feas,
> que aunque de éstas mates muchas
> siempre quedará cosecha? (259)

From the speaker's attitude toward his reader, it is evident that the tone of this poem is quite virulent. The same is true of all the remaining poems of this group, since almost all of them have doctors as their implicit receivers. Because of the underlying levels of meaning, this caustic tone takes on a more satirical nature which lessens the seriousness with which it is viewed by the reader. Nonetheless, the tone of most of these poems is acrimonious almost to excess.

Caviedes' satires and general attacks on doctors have a diversity of situations, as the subjects of the individual poems attest. Some are contrived situations and are undoubtedly fictional creations of the poet's imagination, while others are quite rational and could easily be based on actual happenings. In the previously mentioned "Loa" (259-262) there is presented what might well have been a real and not fictitious situation. In this and many other poems, one finds that the initial and basic situation is soon left in the background and has little or no importance for the development of the poem, since it serves only as a springboard from which the poet launches his personal attacks against a doctor or group of doctors. Another poem which has a definitely factual foundation is "A Machuca por su nombramiento de médico de la Inquisición" (264-265), as well as two different poems to Dr. Bermejo on the occasions of his being named rector of the University (93) and Protomédico de Hacienda (305-311). The "Coloquio que tuvo con la Muerte un médico estando enfermo de riesgo" (230-233) and the "Pregunta que hacen los alguaciles y escribanos, temerosos de que se les pegue a los gatos la peste de los perros" (303-305), along with several other poems, are undoubtedly of fictional origin. At least there is no known historical basis for assuming that they are anything more than creations of the poet's imagination.

Hardly a single poem can be mentioned which fully develops the situation described or hinted at in the long involved titles given the poems. The fact that Caviedes does not adhere unerringly to the basic situation presented alleviates what might be a monotonous subject. What could seem more unpoetic than a work dealing exclusively with the removal by Pedro de Utrilla of a huge kidney stone from a woman (243-246) or the fact that there were indiscreet rumblings of stomachs during the speech that Dr. Fuentidueñas delivered in acceptance of his degree of Bachiller in the Facultad de Matanza (233-234)?

These somewhat ridiculous situations serve only to provide a starting point from which the poet can initiate his ridicule of the people involved and aid in convincing the reader of the stupidity and ineptness of doctors. In these fifty poems only two similar situations are repeated. A *mulato cohetero* (103-104) and an *hijo de sastre* (107) are attacked for having left their profession to become doctors. The other is the occasion of the marriage of Pico de Oro with a rich, old *panadera* (266-268) and the marriage of Doctor del Coto. [2]

---

[2] *Documentos literarios del Perú*, ed. Manuel de Odriozola (Lima, 1873), V, 117-118. Hereafter cited as *Documentos*, or *Doc.* in the text.

In this single group of poems, thirty-two different doctors appear as major characters, while a similar number of less important personages is also to be found. Of these doctors at least twelve have been identified as real persons who lived and practiced medicine in Lima during the second half of the seventeenth century. Dr. Francisco Vargas Machuca, Dr. F. Ramírez, Dr. Avendaño, Dr. Bermejo, Dr. Antonio García, Dr. Pedro de Utrilla, Dr. Melchor Vásquez, Dr. Herrera, Dr. Revilla, Dr. Esplana, Dr. Barco, and Dr. Guerrero are all mentioned in several different sources.[3] Doña Elvira, the only female quack mentioned by Caviedes, is also known as a *curandera* of the epoch.[4] It is very likely, too, that many of the other doctors mentioned by Caviedes were real persons whose lack of professional fame did not allow their names to be recorded by historians. A few are creations of the author as their names seem to indicate. Dr. Pico de Oro, Dr. Corcobado, Dr. Fuentidueñas, and Dr. don Terciana could be nicknames given to real doctors, but it is unlikely since Caviedes never seemed to have any hesitation against making straightforward mention of any of them, as his attacks on such people of influence as Dr. Bermejo, the viceroy's personal physician, and Dr. Machuca, the rector of the University and doctor of the Inquisition, readily attest.

Besides the roles played by Death (personified) and the Hospital of San Andrés, there are two other characters who reappear in Caviedes' works. They are two famous drunkards of the epoch named Piojito and Portugués (275). Although they only receive slight mention in these poems, they are the direct brunt of the poet's satire in others.

All of these poems have the same basic theme of social criticism or hate for doctors and anything associated with them. It should always be understood, however, that this over-all theme is

---

[3] These twelve doctors can be found in the following sources: Juan B. Lastres, *Historia de la medicina peruana: La medicina en el virreinato*, II (Lima, 1951); José Toribio Medina, *La imprenta en Lima (1584-1824)*, II (Santiago, 1904); Hermilio Valdizán, *Apuntes para la bibliografía médica peruana* (Lima, 1928); Luis A. Eguiguren, *Catálogo histórico del claustro de la Universidad de San Marcos (1576-1800)* (Lima, 1912).

[4] Juan B. Lastres, *Historia de la medicina peruana: La medicina en el virreinato* (Lima, 1951), II, 130.

somewhat diminished in intensity by the satirical nature of the works themselves. As mentioned before, Caviedes wanted to show his passionate dislike for doctors as his essential purpose, but he also wanted to make people laugh.

If a general thesis is to be extracted from these poems, there can be only one central thesis — all doctors are murderers and wish only to kill their patients, not cure them. Rare is the situation, indeed, in which a doctor is not directly accused of being a murderer or in which the fact is not alluded to metaphorically. Machuca is called "verdugo en latín" (259), "Matalote, graduado en calaveras" (261), and "doctor de la sepultura" (261). Vásquez is referred to as "nuestro matadero" (*Doc.*, 71) and "Doctor Garrotillo" (263), Yáñez as "don matadura" (240), and doctors in general are referred to as "sangrientos ministros [de la muerte]" (218). Thus, as can easily be seen, the thesis is clear in all of these examples and permeates each poem which deals with doctors.

As might be expected of poetry of the late seventeenth century in Spanish, Caviedes' works are most influenced by the Baroque. Notwithstanding, a close examination of the poems does show that Caviedes is not a completely baroque poet as one might consider the more baroque works of such writers as Góngora, Quevedo, Calderón, or Sor Juana Inés de la Cruz. If Caviedes' works do show a similarity of influence of epoch style to any of the aforementioned, it is without a doubt to Quevedo's works. Although there are some examples of hyperbaton and other complexities of syntax in the poems, they are not common characteristics. In the following examples one sees some elements of hyperbaton:

> ¿Cuántos pensáis que estarán,
> sólo por no haber tenido
> dos pesos para pagarme,
> en aquesta ciudad vivos? (310)

> Que había vaguidos dijo
> de estómago, ¡qué insolencia!
> doscientos le habrán de dar
> azotes, por tal simpleza. (234)

> Melchor Vásquez por delante
> eres, si los ojos curas
> de la cara con punzones,
> y los de atrás con ayudas. (297)

One stylistic feature of Caviedes' poems is the long involved sentence which is occasionally used. In many cases this could be confused with a certain baroque complexity, as is seen in the following example in which the subject of the sentence, *la Muerte*, in the first verse is separated from its predicate, *ha acordado aconsejar*, by seven lines of verse:

> la Muerte, como quien sabe
> el modo de los fracasos,
> pues todo morir es uno
> de médicos y de dardos,
> conociendo que estos mares
> los infestan los corsarios,
> y que son gastos enormes
> muralla, escuadra y soldados,
> ha acordado aconsejar
> en tan delicado caso
> a Vuecencia, que embarque
> a todos los boticarios... (250)

Here, again, it must be noted that the poet's works do not have such involved sentences as a rule, but as the occasional exception.

Very few, if any, *cultismos* are to be found in this group of poems and there are few classical allusions. Almost all of the allusions are made to famous physicians and figures in the field of medicine such as Galen, Avicenna, and Hippocrates. One poem does not conform to this general principle This is the "Romance jocoserio..." (312-322) in which there is a large number of allusions to men of medicine as well as a list of thirty classical, Biblical, and historical figures from Isaiah, Socrates, and Seneca to Almanzor and Alfonso el Sabio. Their mention is necessitated by the fact that Caviedes has returned to the past in order to cite the views of others who support his thesis that doctors are stupid murderers.

The number of Latinisms is also limited. Almost all are taken directly from medical aphorisms — and they are usually employed in the same contexts within the works — as one sees in the following example:

> ...y es
> triaca del veneno dicho,
> porque *contraria, contrariis*
> *curantur* que es aforismo
> médico... (256)

The question which arises, then, is what is baroque about Caviedes' works if they are not essentially *gongorino* or *culterano?* In this group of poems at least they are largely *conceptista*. Since one of the basic elements of these poems is satire, it is not surprising that there are many examples of *conceptismo* and *juegos de palabras* in each poem. Through the use of *conceptismo* the poet is able to convey several levels of meaning with a single word or phrase. It is often found that *conceptismo* is employed in lewd or risqué references as in the following quotation:

> Por punzar las cataratas
> la niña del ojo punzas,
> pero, ¿quién en la ocasión
> punzar las niñas rehusa? (297)

The obvious reference made here is to the fact that the doctor in question not only destroys the cataracts, but also the pupil of the eye, while the scope of his interest in the *niña del ojo* is enlarged to include the *niña* as well.

Conceptismo is also found in references to physical defects of various people. This interest in the grotesque and deformed is a commonly found characteristic in baroque painting as well as literature. In the following quotation one sees references to Dr. Corcobado's hunchback:

> Seré el doctor *Corcobado*
> que, con emplastos y apodos,
> birla mucho más que todos
> porque este mata doblado.
> Y aunque siempre anda gibado
> en las espaldas y pecho,
> este médico mal hecho
> en el criminoso trato,

>   si cura cual garabate
>   a matar sale derecho. (232)

The use of *conceptismo* in this particular situation is found to an even greater extent in the poems dealing specifically with satires of physical deformities.

Examples of *conceptismo* are often combined with or found in poems in which *juegos de palabras* abound. At times the *juego* involves a variety of combinations of the same words, as in this example:

>   Doctor de tápalo todo
>   no inventó Pedro Urdemalas [5]
>   mas quien te tapara un todo
>   si tu todo no te tapa. (271)

At other times it is simply a play on one word, as in the following example, in which the meaning of cure and priest is suggested by the word *cura(s)*:

>   Aun más que de gran parroquia
>   tiene esta iglesia resabios,
>   pues la ha hecho de mil curas,
>   cuando en la mayor hay cuatro. (242)

The poet refers to the fact that the church was built by money earned by a doctor as medical fees. The *mil curas* refers to the many cases or fees that the doctor collected to build it, while the poet suggests that only four *curas* (priests) are usually found in the major churches. In yet another example the understanding of what is meant hinges on the different meanings of *mosca*, which refers alike to the insect and the popular term for money:

>   También, como araña, tiendes
>   telas que haces pegajosas
>   de médicos, que se tejen
>   del hilo de tu ponzoña,
>   para coger el enfermo

---

[5] The allusion is quite possibly to the character made famous by Cervantes in his *Comedia famosa de Pedro de Urdemalas*.

luego que el médico toca,
pues en él cual mosca muere,
porque éstos matan por mosca. (222-223)

All of these basic characteristics, especially the *conceptismo* together with the *juegos de palabras,* show Caviedes to be most akin to the *conceptista* poets of the Baroque, especially Quevedo. Although some elements of *culteranismo* or *gongorismo* are to be found in these poems, they are not nearly so strong that they overshadow the stronger elements of *conceptismo.*

It is not surprising to find that a large portion of the metaphors employed in these poems are concerned with doctors, since they are the characters involved in the situations presented. There are approximately one hundred different metaphorical allusions to them. Practically all are either connected to the science of medicine or to Death, which according to Caviedes is the leader or demigod of all doctors. Others are based on allusions to figures in the field of medical history. At times, however, there is a mixture of imagery in the metaphors in keeping with the general scheme of images involved in a particular poem. One finds that Dr. Machuca is called "doctor don Tabardillo" (256), "verdugo en latín" (259), "loro de Avicena" (260), "matalote, graduado en calaveras" (261), "Doctor de la sepultura" (261), and "licenciado de la huesa" (261); Dr. Yáñez is "don matadura" (240), "ripio fatal de la Muerte" (270), and "pronóstico de desgracias" (270); Dr. Vásquez is a "tonto presumido" (*Doc.*, 70), "nuestro matadero" (*Doc.*, 71), "Doctor Garrotillo" (263), "Cupido de medicina" (297), "médico Aquilón" (297), and "cuervo curandero" (297); Dr. Bermejo is a "protoverdugo" (305) and "volcán graduado en los ataques de la salud" (305); Dr. Fuentidueñas is a "médico matasiete" (233); Dr. Avendaño is a "catedrático de sepulturas funestas", "doctor Terciana", "cimarrón de la medicina", "matante a diestra y siniestra", and "señor de horca y cuchillo" (234); and doctors in general are referred to as "bachiller *nemini parco*" (225), "licenciado ballestero" (226), "mis carneros [de la Muerte]" (226), "impulsos de tu guadaña [de la Muerte]" (223), "vuestros soldados [de la Muerte]" (225), and "campeones señalados [de la Muerte]" (252). In the case of the *mulato cohetero* and the *hijo de sastre* who became doctors, the former is called "perdiguero o podenco de la Muerte", "docto en cohetes", and "sabio en triquitraques" (103), while the latter is simply a "físico idiota" (107).

Three characters who are referred to metaphorically and who deserve individual attention are Pedro de Utrilla, *el cachorro* (so called to distinguish him from his father), Dr. Corcobado, and Dr. Cordillera. They represent three cases apart from the general characteristics of metaphorical allusions to doctors. Pedro de Utrilla is attacked by Caviedes because he is a mulatto as well as a doctor. Most of the references to Utrilla use or allude to the color black in some way as seen in the following:

> El licenciado Morcilla
> y bachiller Chimenea;
> catedrático de Ollín
> y graduado en la Guinea;
> doctor de la Cámara oscura
> del rey congo de Norieza,
> cuando ha comido morcilla,
> que es la Cámara morena;
> condesillo de Galeno;
> ... ...
> perdiguero de la caza
> de su criminal ballesta,
> ... ...
> cóndor de la cirujía
> que, por comer de tragedia,
> de toda la carne viva
> sueles hacer carne muerta;
> ... ...
> tumba sensible que viste,
> por adentro y por afuera,
> de negro luto forrada,
> bayeta sobre bayeta;
> responso de cocobolo,
> manga de cruz con que entierran,
> cabo de año de azabache,
> duelo mandinga de negras;
> paño de entierro enrollado
> ... ...
> noche de uno de Noviembre,
> puesto que se trata en ella
> de finados, como aqueste
> mata-físico tinieblas. (243-244)

Dr. Corcobado is attacked in metaphors alluding to his hunchback with images comparing him to animals and birds, as one sees in the following quotations:

>Oye, corcobado físico
>De mi corcobado cántico
>Los agraviados esdrújulos,
>Loa de un dos veces sátiro.
>A tí *quircuncho* de médicos
>Y licenciado galápago,
>Mojiganga de la física,
>Tuerto en derechos de párroco. (*Doc.*, 46)

>Mono de la medicina,
>Gimió de los curanderos,
>Espantajo de barberos,
>Médico de melecina,
>Con más comba que bocina
>Que esa tu corcoba encierra. (*Doc.*, 47)

In the first example it would seem that even the final *esdrújulos* serve to augment the suggestion and allusión to Dr. Corcobado's deformity by making a jerky abruptness at the end of each verse.

Besides the obvious allusions to geographical landmarks and natural phenomena in the metaphors referring to Dr. Cordillera, the poet has carried the same imagery throughout the poem, thus giving it a certain density which it might not have had, if the images had been more diversified, as one sees illustrated in the following quotation:

>El bachiller Cordillera,
>licenciado Guadarrama,
>doctor puna de los Lipes,
>y médico Pariacaca,
>sierra de la medicina
>y graduado por la escarcha,
>carámbano con golilla,
>seco granizo con barbas,
>me visitó en un achaque
>para helarme las entrañas
>con mil recetas diciembres
>que tirito de nombrarlas.
>Díjele: turbión albéitar,

¿en qué Galeno garrafa,
en qué nevado Avicena
o en cuál Hipócrates aura,
aprendistes a matar
con tus curas madrugadas
y récipes garrapiñas,
que son betún, pues se mascan?
¿En qué charcos estudiaste,
en qué Genil o Jarama
practicaste, o qué Tajo
te enseñó esas cuchilladas? (273-274)

Whenever allusions are made to the genitalia or to indecent acts, they are always carefully cloaked in metaphorical language. Thus, the allusion becomes less offensive to the reader than a direct reference, and it would seem justifiable to assert that in most cases they in no way detract from the artistic merit of a poem. In the following quotation there is a metaphorical allusion to the female genitalia when the poet describes one of Pedro de Utrilla's cures in which he took a large kidney stone from a woman:

A una mujer abrió en Lima
por la parte que no cierra
y una piedra le sacó
que pesaba libra y media. (245)

In the "Fe de erratas", of the initial portion of the *Diente del Parnaso*, Caviedes gives a list of words which should be substituted for others in the texts of the poems. These terms in themselves can be considered as a primary basis for metaphorical allusions to doctors and medical practices which are commonly found in the poems:

En cuantas partes dijere
Doctor, el libro, está atento;
porque allí has de leer *verdugo*,
aunque éste es un poco menos.
Donde dijere *receta*
dirás *estoque*, por ello;
pues estoque y verduguillo
todo viene a ser lo mesmo.
Donde dijere *sangría*

has de leer luego *degüello,*
y *cuchillo* leerás donde
dijere *medicamento.*
Adonde dijere *purga*
leerás—*dio fin el enfermo;*
y a donde *remedio* diga
leerás *muerte sin remedio.*
Donde dice *practicante*
leerás, sin más fundamento,
sentencia de muerte injusta
por culpas de mi dinero.
Y con aquestas erratas
quedará fielmente impreso
porque corresponde a las
muertes de su matadero. (213)

The imagery of this group of poems is largely visual with only an occasional auditory or thermic image being used. A large portion of the images have to do with medicine, doctors, and medical practices. One factor, however, does serve to differentiate and make many of the images stand apart through a combination of medical and arms imagery. Since doctors are generally considered by Caviedes to be Death's soldiers, the poet has mixed medical and bellicose images in order to give a more diversified kind of visual image. In a reference to Dr. Yáñez the poet says:

Corta una receta tuya,
que es más que hoja toledana,
lo que va de un yerro solo
a muchos de más de marca.
Tan valiente eres en purgas,
que, cuando una desenvainas,
das tanto temor que al punto
tienen la muerte tragada. (270)

The example shows how a *receta* is likened to a sword and the *purga* is also unsheathed by the doctor as he would a sword.

In the "Coloquio que tuvo con la Muerte un médico estando enfermo de riesgo" (230-233), one finds the personification of Death appearing in the poem surrounded by arms imagery.

Repara que soy tu amigo,
y que de tus tiros tuertos

> en mí tienes los aciertos;
> ....
> pues, con purgas y con untos,
> damos a tu hoz asuntos
> para que llenes los trojes,
> ....
> Pobre, ociosa y desvalida
> quedarás en esta suerte,
> sin que tu aljaba concierte,
> siendo en tan grande mancilla
> una pobre muertecilla
> o Muerte de mala muerte.
> ....
> Porque soles ni desmanes,
> la suegra y suegro peor,
> fruta y nieve sin licor,
> bala, estocadas y canto,
> no matan al año tanto
> como el médico mejor. (230-231)

Another poem which deserves special mention for its continuity of bellicose and medical imagery is the "Memorial que da la Muerte al Virrey..." (250-252). On addressing the Viceroy, Duque de la Palata, on the subject of the pirates who were attacking Peru's coastal area at the time, Death advises the following in combating them:

> La Muerte...
> ha acordado aconsejar
> en tan delicado caso
> a Vuecencia, que embarque
> a todos los boticarios,
> barberos y curanderos
> y, en fin, a los matasanos,
> sin exceptuar a ninguno,
> por ser caso averiguado
> que si cada quisque de ellos
> birla al día tres o cuatro
> españoles, cortaráse
> sin médicos este daño,
> se aumentará la milicia,
> y el enemigo al contrario,
> birlándole los infantes
> con purgas y con emplastos.
> Los que mataban en Lima

quedarán ya castigados,
España con la victoria
y la Hacienda Real sin gastos. (250)

Death then continues to liken an entire series of doctors to various kinds of ships and shows how they will solve the Viceroyalty's problem, as one sees in the following quotation from the same poem:

¿Soldados son menester
donde se halla un doctor *Barco*,
que puede abordar a un
bajel de vidas cargado?
... ...
¿Un *Machuca* que, con solo
su gravedad, ha volado
más vidas que una fragata
de fuego en incendios varios?
¿Un *Ramírez*, bravo buque
armado siempre de estragos,
pues tiene mil toneladas
de ignorantes matasanos?
¿Un *Revilla*, que es lijero
bajel de corso tirano,
aunque por tanta obra muerta
había de ser pesado?
¿Una capitana *Elvira*,
que en sí cabalga, bien largos,
cien cañones de jeringa
por cada banda o costado?
... ...
¿Dos fragatones *Utrilla*
por el color embreados
y por la casta, pues pueden
los dos estar amasando?
Los demás que restan son
también pequeñuelos barcos
que hacen, pues visitan poco,
sus muertos de cuando en cuando.
En fin de todas aquestas
naves cargadas de emplastos,
de geringas y de tientas
y polvos confeccionados,
alhucemas y diagridios,
y todos cuantos petardos

> y bombardas las recetas
> nos muestran en sacatrapos,
> ballestas, flechas, machetes,
> tridentes, lanzas y garfios. (251-252)

In a similar attack on Dr. Yáñez in the poem "Al Doctor Yáñez que andaba de color y con espada" (270-271), the poet combines the ideas of sword and playing card to create the images used in the poem.

> Ripio fatal de la muerte,
> pronóstico de desgracias,
> que por matar a dos ases
> has querido usar espada.
> Que eres matador malilla
> parece, si se repara,
> porque a dos espadas juntas
> las llaman el dos de espadas. (270)

Another poem written in reply to a pronouncement made by Dr. Machuca, in which he had urged the elimination of *pepinos* (cucumbers) from the diet of the Indians, utilizes imagery of fruits and vegetables to make fun of doctors. This imagery is carried throughout the poem and gives excellent continuity to the subject. Machuca is the first of a series of doctors to be described by means of this particular technique, as one sees in the following:

> Sólo la pera, en las frutas,
> mata, y aquesto lo firmo
> de cierto, porque Machuca
> para ser introducido,
> trae una pera en la barba
> ... ...
> y así de barba de pera
> mueren más que de pepinos (256)

The direct connection of the *pera* with Machuca is that the style of beard which he evidently wore was popularly called *barba de pera*. As the imagery is continued in the poem, Liseras is likened to a *cohombro*, Francisco Ramírez, to a *zapallo*, Avendaño, to a *camote*, Bermejo and don Lorenzo el Indio, to *yucas*,

Antonio García to an *higo,* Pedro de Utrilla, *el viejo,* to a *berengena,* Pedro de Utrilla *el cachorro,* to a *rábano,* doña Elvira, to a *papaya,* and her son Elviro, to a *badea;* furthermore, the poet adds that they are all "físicas frutas que matan/con venenos y diagridios" and that if any fruit should be destroyed, it should be the seed of these people that he has just named (256-257).

In retrospect it may be said that the imagery used in these poems is for the most part visual and is made up largely of medical images mixed with other types in direct relationship to the themes and situations presented. It would also seem reasonable to assert that many of the better poems are those which show greater ingenuity in different sources of images, but which also have strong continuity because of the use of a basic source of imagery for an individual poem.

Within the various techniques found in these poems, one which seems to be utilized most by the poet in his art is the comparison. In the shorter comparisons the purpose usually seems to be to enhance the point being made by the poem. In an attack against Dr. Machuca the poet uses the following short comparison of Hippocrates and Machuca to emphasize the latter's vanity:

> Muere Hipócrates, y exclama
> que muere cuando comienza
> a saber la Medicina,
> con cien años de experiencia.
> ¡Y vos, apenas nacéis
> cuando pensáis que a la excelsa
> cumbre del saber llegáis
> con mentecata insolencia! (259-260)

On the occasion of Dr. Bermejo's being named Protomédico de Hacienda, the poet compares Bermejo to a local English hangman. Eighty-eight verses of the two hundred ninety in the poem are devoted to a conversation between Bermejo and the *verdugo* through which the poet shows how the tortures of the latter are very similar to those used by Bermejo in his medical practices.

> —Decidme, hermano, ¿qué es horca?
> Y el respondió de improviso:
> —es una junta de tres

> palos—Y Bermejo dijo:
> —Sois un médico ignorante,
> que la junta que hemos dicho
> no es de tres palos, sino
> de tres médicos pollinos.
> —Decidme ¿qué son azotes?
> Y respondió—señor mío,
> los que se dan con la penca.
> Y el otro corrijió:—amigo,
> ventosas y frotaciones. (306)

Another comparison which warrants mention is one comparing the advertising techniques of the tavern owners of the epoch with the methods of recognizing a doctor.

> Y que si el cargo aceptare
> no traiga barbas ni anillo,
> ni guantes, que de doctores
> son signos demostrativos;
> pues como los taberneros
> para decir—aquí hay vino—
> ponen un ramo en la puerta
> que a los borrachos da indicios,
> traiga este médico en las
> barbas un macho cabrío,
> con lo que indique a las gentes
> aquí hay peste y tabardillo. (300)

Although this advertising technique has long since disappeared from the urban areas of Peru, it is still popularly used in the more distant provinces to proclaim the fact that the establishment has *chicha* for sale. One finds also an entire poem based on a comparison of doctors and earthquakes in "Que teman los temblores y no teman los doctores" (292-294).

Uses of parallelisms and enumerations of words and phrases are relatively common in the entire group of poems, as can be seen from a random examination. One such example is the following which contains enumerations and parallelism of dominant words placed at the end of the verse for emphasis:

> Porque aquellos que no pasan
> la cuña de una calilla,
> el pegote de un emplasto,

el punzar de una sangría,
el acíbar de una purga,
las bascas de otras bebidas,
los araños de ventosas,
esponjas de chupar vidas,
no sabrán darle el lugar
que, en las veras y las triscas,
merece mi humilde libro
de aplauso o premio a que aspira. (214-215)

The use of enumerations and parallelisms as a part of the poet's art serves to add to the intensity of the poems by building up the density of imagery. The technique is further worthy of note as a general feature of the poet's style.

Only one real symbol appears in these poems. Its use is of double interest, since the same symbol appears in the *Poema del Cid*, but with a far different significance. The symbol of the *barba* of the doctors is first explained in an attack on Dr. Machuca.

Solo la pera, en las frutas,
mata, y aquesto lo firmo
de cierto, porque Machuca
para ser introducido,
trae una pera en la barba,
con que al vulgo sin aviso
lo provoca a que lo llamen
y los mata inadvertidos;
y así de barba de pera
mueren más que de pepinos. (256)

As has already been explained, the *barba de pera* was a style of beard popular during the epoch, and the *barba* appears repeatedly in the other poems as a symbol of doctors, medical quackery, and death (205, 223, 260, 270, and 300). In another example the poet adds two other identifying marks by which a doctor may be recognized.

Y que si el cargo aceptare
no traiga barbas ni anillo,
ni guantes, que de doctores
son signos demostrativos. (300)

As regards the language of the poems, a few general observations may be made. It has already been noted in the remarks on epoch style that there is no great evidence of *cultismos* in the poems. The few neologisms used are largely verbs manufactured from nouns. In the following example the poet makes a verb from *aforismo:* "y en latín de solecismos/ciegamente aforismea,/aquel intruso Doctor" (233-234). Although there are several lewd and risqué references in the poems, only two scatological remarks appear (235 and *Doc.,* 69). The same is true of words of indigenous origin. Only the Quechua word *chasque* is used in the popular sense of *cartero* (301). An imitation of an Indian's manner of speaking Spanish is used in the poems in which Dr. don Lorenzo, the Indian doctor, speaks. Following is an example of this type of language:

> qui conoce a otro y a uno,
> qui son moy señores mios,
> el toirto y el señor Vásquez,
> hijo de la Doña Elvira,
> y qui sabe qui il Dotor
> porqui el toirto traia
> in so mola, con pirdon
> di osti, assi come digo,
> oltimamente il folano
> qui iba con Llanos so amigo
> con sus nalgas en un mola,
> en las ancas en un sillo... (283)

The example shows that the poet was making a conscious attempt at reproducing speech mannerisms as realistically as possible.

Another language element which stands out more than some of the others is the use of Americanisms. Many are words referring to indigenous plants and animals such as *penca (hoja carnosa de ciertas plantas)* (306), *cocobolo (árbol de la familia de las poligonáceas)* (244), and *quircuincho (armadillo americano)* (235). In other cases the Americanisms are simply words used regionally with different connotations.

As already mentioned in the remarks on features of epoch style, the syntax and general sentence structure used in the poems are not on the whole out of the ordinary. Some cases of complex syntax and hyperbaton are to be found, but they are more the exception than the rule. Many of these examples can be explained in part, however, by the fact that poetic license often demands that general syntactical patterns be altered somewhat by the limitations of verse structure and rhyme.

B. Satire of Other Professions and of Types

Caviedes did not limit his satires exclusively to doctors and medical quacks, but included many other professions together with a diversity of types of people. Poets, painters, actors, clergymen, drunkards, mulattoes, and people with physical deformities are the principal figures satirized; however, hypocrites, scribes, tailors, students, fruit sellers, *pordioseros, alcahuetas, beatas, dueñas,* and *doncellas,* among others, are also mentioned in varying degrees of disdain. Only a few real persons appear in these poems, however. Among these are the drunkards Coto and Piojito (193) and the *pordioseros* Bachán and Juan González (40-43); the latter was more popularly known as Portugués. Also mentioned are Cristóbal de Virués Duarte, an actor who at the end of the century was active in Lima's theaters,[6] and the Conde de la Monclova, a viceroy of the epoch (40).

The one factor which most separates these poems from those dealing with doctors is the lack of vehemence on the part of the poet in his attacks on the various people. There is little or no evidence that the poet rabidly hated or disliked any of them as he did doctors. He simply pokes fun at them, points out their faults, and ridicules them. All the poems have in common the fact that social criticism is found in each of them, but there is no evidence of a recurring thesis condemning them as murderers or even as social outcasts. Neither is there an attempt to create a situation or basic element of action in the majority of the poems. In those where a basic situation does exist, there is no

---

[6] Guillermo Lohmann Villena, *El arte dramático en Lima durante el virreinato* (Madrid, 1945), p. 621.

attempt to develop it—only to use it as a catalyst for initiating another satire of persons or types.

Almost eighty percent of the poems are *romances* with a variety of types of assonance. Predominating among these types are those of "a-o" (six *romances*) and "e-o" (eight *romances*). Ten sonnets with the characteristic ABBA:ABBA rhyme in the quatrains and CDC-DCD in the tercets are also included in the group. Besides the *redondillas* and *cuartetas* found in the *agudas* and *epigramas,* there are two forms which have not previously been seen. The first of these is a *seguidilla* with stanzas of alternating heptasyllabic and pentasyllabic verses with assonance in the latter. The other form heretofore unseen is evident in two poems made up of *versos pareados*. Hendecasyllabic verses are used more predominantly than heptasyllabic in the latter. The couplets are either hendecasyllabic or a combination of hendecasyllabic and heptasyllabic verses with consonantal rhyme, as is seen in the following:

>   Érase un retrato tosco de marido,
>   sobrado de algún corte de Cupido,
>   que amor sastre, por no desperdiciarlo
>   se le antojó casarlo. (162)

The only other strophe introduced is that of a poem of nine *redondillas* of octosyllabic verses and a rhyme scheme of abba, etc. With the exception of the eight sonnets, all of these forms are those ordinarily used when treating subject matter of a popular nature. There are neither metrical nor strophic innovations to be found in any of these poems.

The major portion of the poems in this group are not addressed to any specific person or group of persons. Twenty-four poems are narrated in the third person singular with only sixteen addressed to a specific person in the second person singular. The narrator is omniscient and is completely aware of everything taking place in the world of the work.

At least half of these poems show some salient features of baroque style. Most of the classical allusions are directly connected to the subject matter of individual poems. Apollo is alluded to in works dealing with poets (36, 139, 156, 157, 167, and 208), and

Bacchus is often cited in the poems treating drunkards (155, 156, and 193).

Hyperbole is used as a technique in some situations to give a more exaggerated or grotesque effect to the poems. "A un amigo viejo en su cumpleaños" (175-178) is a completely hyperbolic poem, since from the beginning the friend is compared to Methuselah and other characters from antiquity, and the exaggeration is increased in intensity throughout the work. In one instance the narrator makes the following remark about the old man's age:

> Que viváis unos seis [años] más
> a Dios solo pido y ruego
> y serán cinco mil ocho
> cuatro meses más o menos. (177)

Excessive exaggeration was a common feature in baroque literature and was used successfully by Caviedes to make situations and persons seem even more ridiculous. It is amply evident in the poems satirizing people's deformities. In the following quotation the poet exaggerates the short stature of a hunchback and the height of his wife:

> Para conseguir poder besarla,
> hubo el marido giba de escalarla,
> porque era novia, en fin, tan atalaya
> que por las picaduras de la saya
> el giba la subió hasta la cadera
> y para más subir pidió escalera.
> Ella, viendo así a su amante orillo,
> una trenza ensartó por un carrillo
> por donde tiró al mozo
> como cubo que sacan de algún pozo. (162)

In another poem, reminiscent of Quevedo's sonnet "A una nariz", one sees how the length of a certain don Antonio's nose is exaggerated to ridiculous proportions.

> Nariz mensajera es, puesto
> que embajadas da de ti
> en las visitas, si antes
> te salen a recibir,
> don Antonio viene dicen

y hay tiempo de prevenir
el chocolate una hora antes
que entre tu cuerpo ruin. *(MS. Madrid, 210v)*

Latinisms are found with even greater frequency in these poems than they were in the previously studied group. Most of these words and expressions are taken from Church Latin or are simply clichés, and are easily understood and commonly used in ordinary speech. Expressions such as *requiem in pace, gloria patri,* and *orate frates* are recognizable out of context as terms ordinarily used in the Mass (136).

The sentence structure of this group of poems seems to be less complex than that of the previous group. There are few long complicated sentences and the use of hyperbaton is quite limited. A case of the latter is seen in the title of the poem "Haviendo cobrado doce pesos el canónigo capón de la limosna de unas Missas [sic] en huevos, le salieron hueros" (MS. Madrid, 224r).

Again, the influence of the Baroque is most evident in the use of *conceptismo* and *juegos de palabras*. In the following example there is an obvious play on the word *vino* meaning wine and in the sense of the third person preterite of *venir*:

> Vos con agua por los pies
> y él con vino por los sesos,
> una gran complicación
> se vio en la gala, supuesto
> que ella a su cuerpo no vino,
> ella si vino a su cuerpo
> ajustada al talle vino,
> porque vino al ferreruelo
> cumplido y el gabán vino
> largo y todo vino bueno;
> el calzón tan solamente
> le vino algo imperfecto... (155)

In one sonnet there is also something of a stylistic *juego*. In the initial quatrains there is a certain amount of parallelism and *juego* between the concept of what is being said and the actual development of the poem.

> Para hallar en Palacio estimaciones
> se ha de tener un poco de embustero,

poco y medio de infame linsonjero,
y dos pocos cavales de bufones.
Tres pocos y un poquito de soplones
y cuatro de alcahuetes recaderos,
cinco pocos y un mucho de parleros,
las obras censurando y las acciones. (96)

At least half of the poems have varying degrees of *conceptismo*. In "Haviendo cobrado doce pesos el canónigo capón...", the entire poem is built around the double concept of *huevo* with its generally accepted meaning in English of egg, but with the further connotation of part of the male genitalia. One of the less lewd examples of *conceptismo* from this poem is seen in the following:

Unas misas cobró en huevos
el canónigo castrado;
porque hay misas de Capón
como hay misas de Gallo. *(MS. Madrid, 224r)*

Another example of *conceptismo* is found in "Habiéndole vestido su Excelencia, le dió este segundo memorial en agradecimiento" (154-156). The poem is addressed to an archbishop who had given some clothing to a drunkard. The main pun on which the understanding of the conceit hinges is the word *lobo*, which in Spanish means primarily wolf, but also drunkard as a secondary meaning. The priest is likened to a shepherd and double meanings are found throughout the quotation:

Cuando por Pastor debíais
ser enemigo estupendo
del portugués, que es gran lobo,
le amparáis como a cordero. (155)

Few differences of general technique are noted in a comparison of these poems and those dealing with doctors. One element which is absent, however, is the long series of metaphors with which the poet referred to doctors. Only a few metaphorical allusions to the people being satirized are used. A *guarda* is referred to as "lechuzo cotidiano" and "murciélago de rondas" (193). Mulattoes are "revoltosos conceptos/de amores blancos y tintos" (163) and an "amigo viejo" is referred to as "Evangelio humano" (176), "cartilla vieja" (177), and "mamotreto de siglos" (177). A hunchback is referred to metaphorically as "Melón de capa y espada", "sapo introducido a hombre", "galápago de maridos", and "bragado novio camote" (159). In another case a man's long nose is called a "colmillo de marfil/pardo de los elefantes" (MS. Madrid, 207v).

Most of the imagery is visual with limited evidence of olfactory and thermic images. In the "Pintura de un borracho gracioso", reminiscent of Velasquez' *Los borrachos,* the poet develops a series of visual images built around different parts of the drunkard's phisique and apparel.

>El pelo, como es odre
>trae por adentro
>y por eso no copio
>del lobo un pelo.
>Es su frente preñada
>de calabazo,
>que es apodo que vino
>propio a sus cascos.
>Son sus cejas tan arcos
>como su cuerpo,
>porque está de ordinario
>un iris hecho.
>Son sus ojos dormidos
>por accidente,
>si en mamando las niñas
>luego se duermen.
>Su nariz, chimenea
>de humos de mosto
>sube el vino por ellas
>lo vaporoso.
>A sus mejillas nadie
>llama carrillos,
>porque éstos suben agua,
>aquéllos vino.
>Con su boca asustados
>trae los poetas,
>porque en bocas que chiflan
>tienen su pena.
>Como hipócrita es siempre

> cuelli-torcido,
> porque los odres andan
> del modo mismo.
> Por ropilla una cuba
> al talle pone
> y a sus muslos dos botas
> en los calzones.
> Dos botillas por calzas
> trae en las piernas,
> porque en cosas de vino
> nunca anda en medias. [7]
> Son sus pies con que coma
> dos cucharetas
> porque no ha de ser todo
> para que beba. (158-159)

Another version of this same poem is found in the romance entitled "Pintura de un borracho que se preciaba de poeta" (146-147). The latter is not the artistic equal of the *seguidilla*, primarily because of its lack of development of the basic imagery, which is much more clearly developed in the *seguidilla*.

Imagery involving the color black is again seen in a poem treating mulattoes. Mention is made of "negra la gala", "capa de bayeta", "encaja en lo moreno su gala", "punta a lo negro", "Pardillos", "gala mandinga", and "siglos guineos", which all include the color black or allude to it in some way (178-179).

Thermic and visual images are combined in the following example taken from a poem in which one sees a description of a painter at work:

> Por anteojos de cristal
> al sol un pintor retrata
> quemándose, sin saber
> la razón por qué se abraza.
> Y es que, como los ardientes
> rayos el cristal traspasan,
> los claros de Celia hermosa
> le abrasaban las pestañas. (52-53)

---

[7] There is an obvious pun on the expression *a medias* and *medias* in the sense of stockings.

Only one example of olfactory imagery is seen in these poems and it is certainly not a refined image, but is one seemingly taken from daily experiences:

>   considérannos comiendo
>   olor de los cochifritos
>   que salen del bodegón
>   en olfato de chorizos... (37)

One technique occasionally found in the poems is the use of internal rhyme. It does add a certain amount of musicality to the verses in which it is used, but it is not a commonly encountered characteristic. In the following quotation the poet uses a kind of echo in the fourth verse:

>   Si tuviera esta piedra el acerico
>   que bordándole estoy a toda priesa
>   al padre provincial que me confiesa,
>   fuera en verdad un acerico rico. (131)

Internal rhyme is also seen in the phrases "haciendo cháncharas, máncharas" (210) and "que para cara de viernes" (MS. Madrid, 208r).

The comparison still remains a favorite technique in a large portion of the poems. One comparison which has already been mentioned in the satire of doctors is used again in a similar situation. Reference is made to the comparison of doctors and tavern owners. The same basic comparison is found in "Remedios para ser lo que quisieres" (140-142) and the "Representación de unos comerciantes quiteños contra el doctor Herrera" (300). The underlying meaning is the same, but the comparison is better and more completely developed in the former. It shows that certain stylistic features tend to recur in the poet's works. In the following quotation Caviedes makes an apt comparison of soldiers and poets:

>   Ser soldado y ser poeta
>   en Vuecelencia es preciso,
>   porque Palas y Minerva
>   no son objetos distintos,
>   porque es Palas en las lides

> y Minerva en silogismos
> y así el acero y la pluma
> vienen a ser uno mismo,
> con que se puede decir
> que escribe el alfanje invicto
> de Vuecelencia y la pluma
> hiere escuadras de enemigos. (39)

In another poem a short comparison is made of poems and pearls. It actually seems to be a more cultured comparison than those generally typical of Caviedes' art in this group of poems at least.

> En fin sólo con las perlas
> puedo comparar las coplas,
> que vale más una neta
> que muchas hechas de aljófar. (166)

The poem "Receta que el poeta dió a Liseras para que sanase de la giba" (276-277) is structured completely on comparisons. The poet develops one comparison after another from the beginning of the work to the end. In the following exerpt one sees how this technique is utilized:

> Más doblado que un obispo
> cuando en su obispado espira,
> y más que capa de pobre
> cuando nueva algunos días;
> más que bracelete vueltas;
> más revueltas que una esquina;
> más que un camino de cuestas;
> más que calle de Sevilla;
> más roscas que un panadero;
> más revuelta que las tripas
> y que vara de corchete
> encubierta en la pretina;
> más gradas que cementerio;
> más rincones que cocina;
> más tropezones que han dado
> los muchachos que desvirgan;
> más hinchado que un abad;
> más agachado que espina... (276)

Parallelisms and enumerations are also widely used in these poems. In the following example one sees parallelism of three *esdrújulos:* the second and third, *concótriz* and *espúltriz*, are possibly nonsense words in the same form as the word, *ventrículo,* which they parallel: [8]

> el ventrículo seco y arrugado,
> la concótriz no puede cocer nada,
> y la espúltriz virtud está viciada. (141)

In yet another poem there is considerable parallelism of dominant words and phrases as one sees in the following example selected from it:

> Contra médicos es todo entendido,
> contra vulgo y sus falsas opiniones,
> contra hipócritas y viles santulones,
> y contra la astrología si ha mentido. (106)

Aside from these examples of parallelism and enumerations there are yet others in a large portion of these poems.

In addition to the classical and mythological allusions which have already been mentioned, there is a considerable number of references to Biblical, historical, and literary figures. The major portion of these appear in the poem entitled "Remedios para ser lo que quisieres" (129-145). In the sections entitled "Caballeros chanflones" and "Doctos de chafalonía", Caviedes attacks those who consider themselves greater heroes than the Cid, Hernán Cortés, and Bernardo del Carpio and better writers than Calderón, Lope de Vega, and Cervantes. In this one poem alone, the poet mentions over fifteen such figures. [9]

Besides the use of Latinisms, the only salient lexical elements in these poems are the Americanisms. *Caracha (serna o roña)*

---

[8] From the context it would seem that they are medical terms, but they are not listed in available dictionaries of medical terminology nor in technological dictionaries of any other type.

[9] Bernardo del Carpio, the Cid, the Duque de Alba, Hernán Cortés, Garcilaso (el Inca?), Ponce de León, Aguilar, Pulgar, Aldana, Santa Mariana, Francisco Pizarro, Benalcázar, Quezada, Pedro de Valdivia, Lope de Vega, Calderón, and Cervantes are among those mentioned.

(249), *chichería (tienda donde se vende chicha)* (140), *santulón (devoto con afectación)* (106), *chafalonía (plata que se usa para vajilla)* (138), and *curcuncho (corcovado)* (210), which is of Quechua origin, are all words employed exclusively in Spanish America or with meanings different from those commonly understood in peninsular Spanish. Only one obscene element of vocabulary is found in all of these poems (*Doc.*, 137). An example of an Indian's manner of speaking Spanish is found in the poem entitled "Al mismo asunto en lengua de indio". In the following exerpt from the poem, one sees how the poet has undertaken to recreate this type of speech in order to enhance the reality of the situation:

> Balga il diablo Corcobado
> que osasti también ti casas,
> sin hallar ganga in so doti
> sino solo mojiganga.
> Parici osti jonto al novia
> tan ridondo y ella larga,
> como in los troncos di juego,
> taco bola in misma cama. (161)

Although there are some isolated cases of complex syntax and hyperbaton, there is little evidence in these poems of radical deviations from general syntactical norms.

C. Feminine Satire

Included in this third subdivision of satirical poems are those by Caviedes which deal primarily with women as their subjects. Although the satire of women is biting in most of the works, there are a few which could best be described as jocular or humorous rather than straightforwardly satirical. These have been included here, since they seem more closely related to satire of women than to any other subject. Caviedes was much more kind in his attitude toward women than one might expect after having read some of his other satires. Even women who are unquestionably prostitutes are referred to as *damas* and this allusion is certainly not made pejoratively in most cases.

A few of the women—Fili (210-211), Lisi (53-55), Eufemia (45-46), Paula (202), Inesilla (195-196), Belisa (*Doc.*, 126-129), Arnarda (*Doc.*, 134-137), and Clara (*Doc.*, 209-212)—are mentioned by name in some of the different poems. None appears to have been a real person as is evidenced by the stock names used. A limited variety of types of women are mentioned in the different poems. They include prostitutes, *alcahuetas, mestizas,* and *feas.*

There are only a few situations developed in these poems. Seven are devoted entirely to describing the physical appearances of different women. Two poems which deal with very similar situations describe a woman's fall down the Cerro de San Cristóbal (*Doc.*, 213-216), a hill just across the Rímac River from metropolitan Lima, and how a woman fell from her mule as she was going to Miraflores (MS. Madrid, 117v-120r), formerly a *balneario,* now a district of Lima. Two poems dealing with prostitutes dwell on their professions and the diseased conditions which have led to their being admitted to the Hospital de la Caridad (*Doc.*, 126-129 and 216-218). Other situations involve a woman who is married to a *mercader capón* (MS. Yale-B, 98v-99v), a woman who is suffering from a severe case of diarrhea (*Doc.*, 129-131), another who flirted by showing her feet beneath the hem of her dress (184-186), and an old woman who pulled out one of her remaining teeth to prove that she had them (208).

A greater variety of poetic forms is found in this group than has been seen in any other. As usual, the *romance* is the form which predominates in number over all others. Only one *décima espinela* and two sonnets are found. *Redondillas, cuartetas, quintillas,* and *pareados* make up another third of the poems. One poem of *coplas de pie quebrado* whose stanzas are of three octosyllabic verses and one final tetrasyllabic verse is used (169-170). Two of the three *seguidillas* found in this group of poems are variants of the most common type which is the four verse stanza of alternating heptasyllabic and pentasyllabic verses with assonance in the latter. A less common variation of the basic *seguidilla* is found in "Una pintura en metáfora de los naipes" (50-52). Each stanza is composed of seven heptasyllabic and pentasyllabic verses in a combination of 7-5-7-5:5-7-5. Verses two and four (pentasyllables) have assonance, as does verse seven at times. The second type, found in the "Pintura de una dama que con su hermosura mataba como los médicos" (53-55), is somewhat rare. Its individual stanzas are of seven verses. The first four are octosyllables and the final three are pentasyllables and heptasyllables in a combination of 8-8-8-8:5-7-5. Lines two and four of the octosyllabic verses have assonance with a different assonance rhyme in the two pentasyllabic verses. Tomás Navarro Tomás in his *Métrica española* mentions that this form was used by Sor Juana Inés de la Cruz.[10] It is found in the poem entitled "Letra XXX" and seems to be the only case in which she used this variation.[11] Caviedes was familiar with at least a part of the works of the Mexican poetess, but to say whether or not this is evidence of her influence on the poet would be a hazardous assumption without more proof (32).

In résumé it may be noted that the major portion of the forms utilized are those commonly found in the poems considered thus far. The only strophic innovations are those found in the two variants of the basic *seguidilla*. Apart from a few exceptions, all of the forms are those commonly used when the subject matter is of a popular nature as is the case in these poems satirizing various types of women.

There are no ostensible variations in the poet's point of view in this group of poems. Half of them are directed to specific persons in the second person singular, while the second half is narrated exclusively in the third person singular. The latter, of course, are those in which the work is basically descriptive. The *yo* of the omniscient narrator appears in twelve poems, but only in those which are directed to specific persons

Several baroque techniques are also utilized in these poems. Few examples of hyperbaton appear, although there are some instances of complex syntax and deviations from normal syntactical patterns (46, 50, and 51); but these are chiefly brought about by rhyme schemes and are justifiable through poetic license.

---

[10] Tomás Navarro Tomás, *Métrica española* (Syracuse, 1956), p. 276.
[11] *Obras completas de Sor Juana Inés de la Cruz, Villancicos y letras sacras*, ed. Alfonso Méndez Plancarte (Mexico, 1952), II, 214-215.

There is also a marked absence of Latinisms. Only three are used in the group of poems and they are mostly clichés such as *refugium pecatorum* (Doc., 218), *ab initio* (180), and *requiem aeternam* (181).

In the first of two poems in which baroque antitheses are found, the poet describes a syphilitic prostitute whose success in her trade has caused her to end up with a bad *negocio* or venereal disease.

> Muy apretada la tienen
> Porque en contrarios efectos
> Tiene negocio muy malo
> Por tener negocio bueno. *(Doc., 216)*

The antithesis and its meaning in the following quotation are evident from what is contained in the passage alone:

> El amor cobra en dolores
> Lo que le prestó en cosquillas,
> Con que a pagar viene en llanto
> Deuda que contrajo en risa. *(Doc, 127)*

At least half of the poems in this group show some evidence of *conceptismo*. It is most ostensible in those poems which deal with somewhat obscene or risqué subject matter. In the *romance* "A una dama que por serlo paró en la Caridad" (Doc., 126-129), there are several examples of *conceptismo*. Caviedes refers to Venus, the goddess of love, who has caused the lady to fall into her syphilitic state and to "Mercurio", another Roman deity; at the same time he alludes to the fact that mercury was often used as a medical cure for the disease with which the woman is afflicted:

> De su estrella se lamenta
> Porque en luceros peligra,
> Si cuanto causó la Venus
> Con el Mercurio le quitan. *(Doc., 127)*

In the description of a woman's tumble down the Cerro de San Cristóbal, Caviedes has occasion to describe the more intimate parts of her anatomy. In the final two verses of the quotation which is to follow, there are several different meanings of the word *vello*. Phonetically the pronunciation of the word would be the same whether it were *vello* (short, smooth hair on the body) or *bello* (beautiful). In the final line it also takes on the meaning of *verlo* (*vello* by assimilation).

> No mostró Juana ni un pelo
> Por ser lampiño y rapaz.
> Todos volvían a verlo
> Sin hartarse de mirar
> Que no era vello aunque lindo
> Y querían vello más. (*Doc.*, 215)

In another example of *conceptismo*, there is a pun on the word *consejo* meaning both advice and the peninsular organization under whose charge operations were carried out in the New World. The pun also involves the name given to the New World, Las Indias, and the obvious fact that *mestizas* are part Indian and part white.

> Una mestiza consejos
> estaba dando a sus hijas
> que hay de mestizas consejos
> como hay el consejo de Indias. (166)

Although there are several examples of the use of *juegos de palabras,* the various plays on the word *cara* in the *pareados* "A una fea" typify the general use of the technique by the poet.

> Tú no eres cara, Fili desdichada,
> porque de ningún hombre eres amada
> ni a otro sentido cara yo te aprecio,
> porque a todos te das por bajo precio.
> Ni cara en rostro, dando el verte enojos,
> que tu fealdad no tiene cara ni ojos,
> por lo cual y es lo cierto,
> tres veces descarada te concierto.
> Y tres veces no cara, Fili ingrata,
> por fea, aborrecida y por barata.
> Mas, ay, que en lo barato se repara,
> que, por más que lo seas, eres cara. (210-211)

The word *cara* appears six times with at least four different meanings and is also an inherent part of the word *descarada*.

It is used in the sense of face, beauty, something of value, and as loved one.

In the quotation to follow, there is an obvious case of *retruécano*. The poet is speaking of the use of mercury in curing Belisa of her venereal disease. In the phrase "el alma den" the poet alludes to the mines of Almadén in Spain, and continues in the same vein by mentioning Huancavelica which was the site in Peru from which the largest quantities of mercury were obtained during the epoch.

> Venganza es de las estacas,
> Si a sus amantes decía
> El alma den, cuyo azogue
> Le vengó Huancavelica. (*Doc.*, 128)

Two poems, "Retrato de una beldad limense, usando de el común embuste de los patricios de esta ciudad" (195-196) and "Otro a la misma, usando el trueco de ambos abusos de el fingido embuste" (196-197), show some evidence of a baroque stylistic *juego*. Besides their obvious linguistic significance, the poems are *truecos* and *embustes* as the titles indicate, which makes them *juegos* for the sake of *juegos*. In the first of these, Caviedes has orthographically changed the "ll" to "y". Rafael Lapesa has noted that Caviedes' works were the first in Spanish America in which the *yeísmo* definitely appeared.[12]

> Si en su airoso beyo taye
> se yega a ver el barbiyo,
> se hará tal garabatiyo
> que no hay quien no se atocaye.
>
> Es su pie tan pulidiyo,
> tan gayardo y orguyoso,
> tan beyo, tan donairoso,
> que mantiene su puntiyo. (195-196)

---

[12] Rafael Lapesa, *Historia de la lengua española* (New York, 1959), p. 320.

In the second of these two poems, Caviedes reverses the *trueco* and changes the *yeísmo* to *lleísmo* in all the words in which it appears.

> ¿Posible es, mi bella Inésa,
> que tan fatales desmallos
> lleguen a eclipsar los rallos
> de ese sol de tu belleza?
>
> Mas llo prometo ensallarme
> con ansias, sollozos y alles;
> para cuando te desmalles
> saber también desmallarme. (196)

Some of the most interesting aspects of general technique are found in the use of imagery and metaphors in six different poems. These include the "Pintura de una dama en metáfora de astrología" (45-46), "Una pintura en metáfora de los naipes" (50-52), "Pintura de una dama en seguidillas" (49-50), "Pintura de una dama que con su hermosura mataba como los médicos" (53-55), "Retrato de una beldad limense..." (195-196), and the "Pintura de una fea buscona en metáfora de guerra" (169-170). Though different in form, all of them have the same basic internal structure. The poet describes a woman in each poem. He begins with the hair, then goes on down the body describing — *frente, cejas, ojos, nariz, mejilla, boca, garganta, pecho, manos, talle, piernas,* and *pie*. This same general order of description is followed in all of the poems with the exception of the last-mentioned which follows a reverse order of development. In it the poet begins with the feet and moves upward to the hair in his description. It might be supposed that the reason for this comes from the fact that in it he is describing a *fea buscona,* and in the other five the descriptions of young, attractive women are given. It cannot be denied that the physiognomy is more aesthetically appealing as a rule than the feet; therefore, the poet begins with the less appealing aspects of the old woman's physique to give additional emphasis to her displeasing appearance.

It is interesting to note the different types of metaphors and imagery used in describing the various aspects of the women's physiques in the six poems. In the following quotations from the first of these poems, one sees how the poet uses imagery and metaphors based on astrology:

> fatalidades anuncia
> suelta la trenza del pelo,
> cometa que por cabeza
> tiene un precioso lucero,
> pero su frente graciosa,
> pedazo de firmamento,
> con los iris de las cejas,
> sale derogando agüeros;
> sus dos luceros mezclaron
> en los ojos Marte y Venus,
> la vida dan apacibles
> y saben matar severos... (46)

In the poem "Una pintura en metáfora de los naipes", the principal images and metaphors all have to do with card games. They are probably the most difficult of all to understand of those found in these poems, since many of the games no longer exist as such. In the following quotation, the two games mentioned are *cientos* and *juego del Rey dormido;* also the word *capote* refers to a player's luck, and *descartar* is used as a part of card playing terminology:

> A los cientos tu frente
> se está jugando
> si éste es juego en que gastan
> muy grande espacio.
> Y das capotes
> de tu ceño, que abrasan
> los jugadores.
> ... ...
> Son los ojos el juego
> del Rey dormido,
> que de las vidas triunfan
> a juego visto;
> si matadores
> te descartas de muchos
> para que roben. (50-51)

The "Pintura de una dama en seguidillas" has the most aristocratic imagery of any poem yet considered in this group. *Oro*, *nácar, azabache, rubí, nieve,* and *jazmín* are some of the more exotic images used in the poem.

>   Víboras de azabache
>   son arqueadas
>   las cejas, que parece
>   que a todos faltan.
>   ... ...
>   El rubí con tus labios
>   juega lo fino
>   y le ganan con darte
>   los dos partidos.
>   De la nieve del cuello
>   que el sol desata,
>   en tu pecho condensas
>   dos pollas blancas. (49-50)

The "Retrato de una beldad limense..." is very similar to the previously mentioned poem in that its imagery also is aristocratic and exotic. In the following quotation one sees how the poet describes the *boca* and *mano* of one of Lima's beauties:

>   Su boca, sin que sea puya,
>   joya tan beya atesora
>   que en coral aljófar yora
>   o en rubí perlas arruya.
>
>   Es su mano un juguetiyo
>   de cristal, tan liso y vano,
>   que el alabastro es viyano
>   para poder competiyo. (195)

Doctors often reappear in other poems, if not as the central figures, then as a means of comparison, as they are used in the "Pintura de una dama que con su hermosura mataba como los médicos". In the following quotation from this poem, Caviedes shows how the different parts of Lisi's body are like the doctors he so often satirized:

>   Tu frente es Yáñez, que mata
>   despacio por el ingreso,
>   si con especies de plata
>   mata tanto como el mesmo.

> Pero se advierte
> que allanan sus espacios
> muerte más breve.
> ... ...
> Por ser grandes matadores
> en tus ojos estoy viendo
> al uno y al otro Utrilla,
> que los dos también son negros.
> Teniendo en ellos
> municiones y tiros
> y perdigueros.
> Por ser azucena y rosa,
> nariz y mejilla, pienso
> que Miguel López de Prado
> me dé en sus flores veneno.
> Si matan bellas
> con jarabes de rosas
> y de mosquetas. (53-54)

The *fea buscona* described by the poet does not fare nearly so well as the other women, as one can clearly see in the bellicose metaphors and imagery which are utilized in picturing her. In the following stanzas one sees how the woman's face, hair, nose, and eyebrows are pictured through images associated with war terms:

> Adarga con mascarón
> es tu cara sin afeite
> y los cabellos de almagre
>   dos broqueles.
> La nariz es sacatrapo
> que el garabato que tiene
> no saca telas, sino
>   con que remiendes.
> Pólvora te falta, mas
> en tí hay algo de qué hacerse,
> que del carbón de las cejas,
>   bien se puede. (170)

It is also interesting to note how the poet referred to undescribable parts of the female anatomy in three of the poems. In all three cases figurative language is a heavy veil through which the metaphorical allusions and images manage to shine. In the first of these three quotations, the poet speaks of the "signo hermoso de virgo"; in the second he mentions "lo que el amor anhela"; and in the third he speaks of "Lo que el recato [modestia] oculta".

> el signo hermoso de virgo,
> astrólogo considero
> que sigue, pero aquí sombras
> pinta el pincel del respeto. (46)
>
> Lo que el amor anhela
> no tiene juego
> porque tú no me dejas
> jugar con ello
> y así lo guardas,
> que no es juego tendido
> lo que recatas. (52)
>
> Lo que el recato oculta
> no he de pintarlo,
> para ver si en aquesto
> doy algún salto. (50)

The contrast which can be noted among the references made in the previous quotation and those found in other poems is astounding. In two of the poems, both dealing with Anarda, a prostitute, the poet has occasion to refer to the female genitalia. In both poems he makes this allusion by using the image of a bell. In the following quotation from a poem in which Caviedes says that Anarda is suffering from the *mal francés* because of her promiscuity, one sees how this image is employed:

> Dicen que la campanilla
> Sin remedio se le cae
> O se le raja, a los golpes
> De tanto badajear. (*Doc.*, 135-136)

In the second of these examples in which a similar image is used, the poet is describing what was seen when Anarda fell from the mule on which she was riding to Miraflores, as one sees in the following quotation:

> La vuelta de la campana
> dio Anarda, y si no sonó

fue por faltar a su llaga
el badajo en la ocasión. *(MS. Madrid, 117v)*

In the *romance* written "A una dama que rodó del Cerro de San Cristóbal", the poet develops a long series of allusions to the same subject. Although it might be argued that the allusions are pornographic, one cannot help but admire the poet's ingenuity and artistry in making this description.

> Al caer mostró por donde
> Suele el pepino amargar,
> Que es por donde el melón huele
> Y las demás hieden más.
> En tanto cielo mostró
> Las causas de tempestad,
> Por donde llueve y por donde
> A veces suele tronar.
> Descubrió Juana, cayendo,
> Lo que por la honestidad
> Nadie lo puede escribir
> Aunque se puede contar.
> Paraíso en que se libran
> Las sucesiones de Adán,
> Por donde heredamos todos
> El pecado original.
> El sol la vino a dar donde
> Dicen que a nadie le da
> Aunque las cosas de Juana
> Tienen poca soledad. *(Doc., 214)*

A few other examples of this type of allusion, which lack the artistry of the one just quoted, are more direct in their references to personal parts of the body (*Doc.*, 129-131 and 213-216). In the "Romance alevoso a las seguidillas de una dama", Caviedes mentions the fact that he may be censured for writing on such subjects, but he discards the idea when he says:

> Perdonad de este romance
> El ser puerco por servicio,
> Que a ser puerco y muerto no
> Lo aplaudiérais de cochino.
> Y pues gustáis del humor
> Vuestro, yo gusto del mío;

Que tengo cursos de versos
Y de ellos estoy ahito. (*Doc.*, 131)

Among the other techniques utilized in these poems are a few examples of the use of parallelism. In the following two quotations, one sees the use of parallelism of dominant words and phrases as well as parallelism of concept:

Como dos luceros beyos
son los ojos dos estreyas,
más que el alba hermosas eyas,
más que el sol briyantes eyos. (195)

Todas las mujeres mandan
sobre lo que dan los hombres,
por eso ellas son las donas,
por eso ellos son los dones. (201)

It may also be noted in the first of these two quotations that the poet makes good use of the comparison technique also.

Long series of enumerations are not so evident in these poems as they were in the previously studied groups. Only in one of the *agudas* is the enumerative technique used to any extent.

No teme Paula al francés,
al portugués, al romano,
al inglés, al persa, al medo,
solamente teme al Parto. (202)

Besides the series of phrases, there is a somewhat obscure pun on the word *Parto* which refers not only to childbirth, but also to the inhabitants of the ancient empire of Parthia.

Alliteration is another technique which is used in these poems at times. It appears in "pinta el pincel del respeto" (46) and again in "por ser donde/tanto apuntero apuntó" (MS Madrid, 118r). It is not a technique which appears excessively, however, in any of the poems under consideration at this time.

Onomatopeia is also used in two different poems. In both, however, it is the same onomatopoetic expression which appears in the words *tris* and *tras,* as one sees in the two quotations which follow:

> Que fue en un tris la caída
> Y fue la vista en un tras. *(Doc., 214)*
>
> La vida estaba en un tris
> Y en un tras, porque el peligro
> De tristrás era igualado
> A las nueces por el ruido. *(Doc., 130)*

The echo technique sometimes employed in internal rhyme is also evident in three different cases. In the following quotation there is an echo in the words *plata/mata, caballo ballo,* and *hallo llo:* "si con especies de plata/mata tanto como el mesmo" (53), "te asustó el caballo ballo" (196), and "y que tu fuerza hallo llo" (196).

Within the vocabulary utilized in this group of poems, a few lexical elements stand out. As in the other poems already examined, there are some Americanisms. One sees a regional use of *crucero del sur* (46) referring to the constellation *Cruz del sur* and *mor[r]isqueta (mueca o gesto ridículo)* (196) is used with a meaning different from that commonly understood in Spain. One Gallicism, *monsiures (Doc.,* 135), is found in a poem dealing with the *mal francés* of a prostitute. Only one obscene element of vocabulary is used in the entire group of poems (MS. Madrid, 118v).

One linguistic phenomenon worthy of note is the confusion of *tú* and *vos* which has resulted in the form *-stes* for the second person singular, preterite tense. Caviedes is not consistent in using this form as a brief examination of his poems easily shows. It does appear, however, at times as in *fuistes* (109). The form comes from a confusion of the use of the second person plural and the second person singular forms of the preterite, according to Rafael Lapesa in his *Historia de la lengua española*.[13] Ample evidence has already been given of the poet's use of the *yeísmo* in the "Retrato de una beldad limense..." (195-196) in which he shows orthographically a peculiarity of the speech habits of the people in Lima during the epoch.

---

[13] Lapesa, pp. 357-358.

The one hundred thirty-two poems which have been considered in the three sections of this chapter show many basic similarities as well as some inherent differences. The most apparent factor common to all of these works is satire, which is directed against people from all levels of society. The poet's most vehement tirades are against the members of the medical profession, but other professionals and social types are also attacked. The entire group of poems could aptly be described as poetry of social criticism, since few people from society's different strata escape the poet's barbs unscathed. Ribald humor is quite often an inherent and integral part of this satire and social criticism.

There is some tendency on the part of the poet to use real and not fictional characters within the world of the work. It has been noted that many of the doctors and a few of the other professionals were Caviedes' contemporaries and compatriots, and in a few cases they might well have been social or professional acquaintances. In contrast with the former, all of the women mentioned in these satires are evidently fictional creations.

It has been noted that there is little attempt made to present a well developed situation in any of these poems. Those which do exist are usually ridiculous creations of the poet's ingenuity and have only one purpose—to serve as a springboard or catalyst for launching or initiating a satirical attack against some person or group of persons.

The attitude of the poet toward his subject matter is what gives many of the works such an acrimonious tone. In at least one-half of the poems the narrator directly addresses a specific person. When such is not the case and a third person descriptive technique is used, the resulting lack of vehemence serves to give a more subdued tone to the poem. In contrasting the satires of doctors and women, this is especially true, since the poet's attitude toward females is considerably more benign than toward medical men.

The most predominant and recurring theme, especially in the satires of doctors, is hate or strong dislike for all members of the medical profession. Coupled to the former is a preoccupation with death which is often a secondary theme. The only ostensible thesis is the condemnation of all doctors as murderers and Death's handymen.

Exactly one-half of the poems considered in this chapter are *romances*. Following in frequency are sixteen sonnets and eleven *décimas espinelas*. *Seguidillas, letrillas, pareados, coplas de pie quebrado, quintillas,* and *redondillas* are used occasionally. Twenty-six *agudas* and *epigramas* are included in the various subdivisions. They are all one stanza poems of a single *quintilla, redondilla,* or *cuarteta*. Because Caviedes is dealing with popular subject matter and with satire, the vast majority of the forms are those which best lend themselves to these two factors.

Baroque features of epoch style are apparent in the vast majority of these works. Although *culteranismo* is not necessarily an integral part of the poems under consideration in this chapter, hyperbaton and some stylistic syntactical complexities are found primarily in the satires of doctors and medical quacks. Classical and mythological allusions are few, but are used occasionally. The most obvious baroque influence is seen in the *conceptismo* employed with *juegos de palabras* in a major portion of the poems of each of these three sections. Because of the satirical nature of the poems, the use of *conceptismo* and *juegos de palabras* serves to augment and intensify the effect of the satire. Latinisms, especially those from medical terminology and the Mass, are used as are antitheses, stylistic *juegos,* and hyperbole. The latter technique is most evident in the poems which satirize physical deformities and abnormalities.

The most salient of the poetic techniques are the metaphors and imagery. Worthy of special note are the elaborate metaphors utilized in the satires of doctors and the jocular descriptions of women. In all but a few of the poems, the imagery used seems to be drawn from the poet's daily life. Imagery of fruits, vegetables, other flora and fauna, maritime vessels, implements of war, card games, astrology, and medical paraphernalia are found in abundance. In a small number of poems dealing with women, one does find evidence of aristocratic and exotic imagery, but this is not a common characteristic of the poet's art in these works at least. Besides predominantly visual imagery, one does find others based on the senses of smell and touch.

Parallelisms, long involved comparisons, and enumerations are the techniques most utilized by the poet. The latter is of special importance, since it enables the poet to intensify the biting attacks being made against people. Other techniques found at times include alliteration, onomatopeia, internal rhyme, personification, and some symbolism. The latter is not a constant technique, although one recurring symbol is found. This is the *barba de pera* of the doctors which is pregnant with secondary meaning and symbolizes medical ineptness, sickness, and even death.

The most conspicuous lexical features are the Americanisms, scatological and obscene words, the large vocabulary of medical terms, and an occasional, but rare Gallicism or neologism. Other ostensible linguistic features are the regional use of the second person singular, preterite tense and the *yeísmo* which is in evidence at times. Aside from a few examples of hyperbaton and syntactical complexities, especially in the satires of doctors, one does not note an overabundance of deviations from normally accepted usage in sentence structure and general syntax. Most of the syntactical complexities found can be explained as a result of poetic expediency.

The poems which have been considered in this chapter are without a doubt the most representative of Caviedes' art. The intensity and sincerity of the poet's satirical attacks against the people in these works are perhaps the most noteworthy of their aesthetic features. It is not intended that one should accept each of the poems in this group as a perfect example of Caviedes' poetic art, since these remarks are based on the entire group and not just on individual poems. As in any artist's creations, some works are better and more appealing than others; and such inconsistencies are certainly found in Caviedes' works. It is easy to see how these poems have largely overshadowed the others in importance, but it would be fallacious to consider only these works as representative of the poet's art when there are other important aspects which certainly cannot be disregarded.

Chapter VI

FORMS OF RELIGIOUS POETRY

The thirty-two poems to be considered in this chapter form a distinct and little studied part of Caviedes' poetic production. The reason that these works, which are based on religious themes and subjects, have not been adequately studied to the present is due primarily to the fact that many of them were not brought to light until 1945, when Luis Fabio Xammar, a Peruvian scholar, published portions of an unknown manuscript of the poet's works.[1] Too, these poems have since been largely overshadowed by the more popular nature of the satirical works. It actually comes as something of a surprise to find that the jocular and often risqué Caviedes of the *Diente del Parnaso* has so contrasting an aspect in his poetic repertoire. It is not uncommon, however, to find poetry of a religious nature among the works of a writer of that epoch whose major productions seem to be anything but religious. Well-known are the cases of Lope de Vega and Francisco de Quevedo whose art as poets includes a noteworthy production of works of a religious nature.

As might be expected from poems dealing with religious themes and subject matter, the characters in them are those directly connected with Christianity. Most of these poems deal with God, Jesus Christ, and the Virgin Mary. Also mentioned are San Miguel, San Atanasio, and San Antonio Abad. Lucifer is mentioned only

---

[1] Luis Fabio Xammar, "Un importante manuscrito de Juan del Valle Caviedes", *Fénix, Revista de la Biblioteca Nacional*, no. 3 (1945), 629-641.

once when the poet speaks of his being an angel who was cast out of Heaven by St. Michael. Other poems do not contain specific characters, either Christian or otherwise.

Since many of these works are meditative and lyric in nature, there is only a limited number of situations presented. Several poems have the Crucifixion as the basic situation; others deal with the Immaculate Conception, the Ascension, the Incarnation, and St. Michael's expulsion of Lucifer from Heaven. In the vast majority of the poems there is only a vague *cuadro* of the penitent *yo* of the narrator in which he beseeches God to forgive him his sinful life. Others are devoted to the adoration of Christ, God, or the Virgin and in them the poet pours forth his great love and adoration.

Spiritual love, especially love of God, Christ, and the Virgin, is the most recurring theme encounted in the entire group of poems. Two secondary themes are fear of God's wrath and a preoccupation over Death. Many times, as in the "Consejos para los mandamientos de la ley de Dios", there is a combination of one or more of these themes (17-19). In the aforementioned poem both love and fear of God are evident. At the end of the *romance* the poet says:

> Amor y temor de Dios
> sobre todo te encomiendo,
> que son de la buena vida,
> los precisos fundamentos. (19)

The theme of death is not evident so much through fear if its coming, but more so from a desire that it come swiftly. At times this almost seems to reflect a suicidal tendency as in the following:

> Tanto aborresco el pecar
> que a ser virtud y no vicio
> matarse, por no ofenderos,
> diera mi vida a un cuchillo.
> Pero sé que en esta acción
> más os ofendo que obligo,
> porque ofendo vuestra sangre
> cuando la propia me quito. (8)

The same attitude toward death is evident again in the sonnet entitled "A Christo crucificado" (23) in which the poet contemplates suicide, but seems to be dissuaded for fear of incurring God's displeasure.

Several different theses are found in these poems, since in part they are of a moral or doctrinal nature. Most are theological truths of which the poet wishes everyone to be aware. Statements such as "God will forgive the most obstinate sinner" (1-8), "Fear of God gives wisdom" (29), "Belief in God must be based on faith and not on proof" (28), and "God makes himself known by keeping himself hidden" (27), are a few of the more commonly encountered doctrinal theses.

On considering the forms used in this religious poetry, one of the first things to be noticed is that there is almost a complete reversal in the kind of strophe used. In the poems of a satirical nature, traditional forms such as the *romance* and the octosyllabic *letrilla* were in greatest evidence; but in these poems, which deal with a more refined and cultured subject matter, the most frequently used form is the sonnet. Twenty-three of the thirty-two poems are sonnets of classical form, while the remainder is made up of *romances* and a single *redondilla*. One other poem of Italianate meters, a *romance heroico*, has the same basic characteristics of the *romance*, but has hendecasyllabic verses with "e-e" assonance. Special note is called to one poem, "Letanías de dos esdrújulas a María santísima" (8-10), in which a somewhat rare combination of meters is used. Since almost every verse in the poem begins and ends with a *palabra esdrújula*, the major portion of them have accented first syllables. These are principally two kinds of verses, *octosílabos dactílicos* (accents on one, four, and seven) and *octosílabos polirrítmicos* (accents on one, five, and seven). Usually one finds that verses with accented first syllables are less frequent than any other type of verse; at least such is true of Caviedes' poems. A further examination of the poem in question, when considering its aspects of epoch style, will show some of the effects achieved by using these meters.

The "Consejos para los mandamientos de la ley de Dios" (17-19), is worthy of special note because of its unique internal structure. Externally it is a *romance* of "e-o" assonance, but internally it is divided into ten unequal parts. Each of these sections is devoted to one of the Ten Commandments. In the first and/or second verses of each section, the poet paraphrases a Commandment and then continues to develop its inherent doctrine throughout the section, as one sees illustrated in the following exerpt from the poem:

> 8.º No mientas, porque Dios ama
> al sencillo y verdadero,
> como que es suma verdad
> y te puso este precepto.
> No murmures ni levantes
> testimonio a nadie, puesto
> que ofende las almas, quien
> les descubre los defectos. (18)

The number of verses in each section ranges from four to twelve except for the Tenth Commandment which contains a longer explanation and a résumé of all that has been said before in the first nine sections.

One other feature of internal structural development employed by Caviedes in these poems is the use of the interrogative construction or rhetorical question. In the "Romance a Jesucristo" (1-8), the poet uses an extended series of interrogatives without giving a single answer to the questions posed. The over-all effect achieved by the use of this technique is to build up the intensity of the poem with a kind of suspense. The poet in this case has been describing and contemplating the Crucifixion and at this point addresses Nature's elements in an apostrophe. He asks why they held back their catastrophic powers at such an opportune time, since it was then that they could have made man feel their wrath for the atrocious act he had just committed, as is seen in the following quotation from the work:

> ¡cielos! ¿estábais dormidos?
> ¿para cuándo son los rayos
> si para entonces no han sido?
> ¿Cómo el eje imaginario
> de ese globo diamantino
> no se tronchó en sus lucientes,
> constantes, eternos, quicios?

elementos, ¿para cuándo
guardábais los torbellinos,
de violencias, que después
no te ha admirado, Dionisio? (2)

The poet continues using this same technique through fifty-six more verses before returning to a third person descriptive technique of development.

The point of view in these works is almost equally divided between two different types. The *yo* of the poet-narrator appears in seventeen different poems and in each of these he is addressing a specific person. God, Christ and the Virgin are the ones to whom the poet most often directs himself, although on one occasion he addresses St. Michael and on two others he addresses the reader. In many cases the attitude of the poet toward those he is addressing is one of humility and humbleness, thus giving something of a penitent tone to the works. In addressing either God, Christ, or the Virgin, Caviedes vasicilates between the use of the second person singular (*tú*) and second person plural (*vos*), although the latter form does predominate. The use of the second person plural usually shows the poet to be more respectful and humble before the addressee than when using the *tú* form, which is reserved for more intimate situations. On at least one occasion in the poem "Reconviniendo la misercordia de Dios" (27-28), God is addressed both as *Vos* and *Tú*.

One aspect of point of view which most separates these poems from others previously studied is the lyric attitude of the poet as seen in some of the one-sided conversations with God, Christ, or the Virgin. In the poetry of social satire, Caviedes usually attacked the people addressed for any number of reasons without actually expressing his own personal feelings lyrically. In these, however, he is more intent on the intimate expression of his emotions to God or some other person. Usually this lyric expression of his emotions to God is in the form of confession, repentance, or adoration.

One of the first things to be observed about this group of poems, when considering aspects of epoch style, is that the *conceptismo* and *juegos de palabras* of the satirical works are less in evidence. It almost seems that Caviedes has ceased to be a *con-*

ceptista and has become a *culterano* in certain respects. Some similarities of epoch style do remain, however. Allusions are plentiful, but in contrast to the medical and classical allusions of the previously studied poems, these are mostly Biblical and Christian. References to "Adán" (3), "Jacob" (9), "Jesé" (9), "Judit" (9), "Sísara" (9), "Ester" (9), "Dálila" (10), "Santo Tomás de Aquino" (22), "Dionisio" (2), and "San Atanasio" (10-13) are of a Biblical and Christian nature, while those to "el Noto" (2), "Aquilón" (2), "Areópago" (26), "Aurora" (9), "Iris" (9), "Belona" (9), "Palas" (9), and "Cupido" (25) are for the most part classical allusions. These references and allusions are in a sense a kind of embellishment of the individual works, since practically every one of them connotes extra and secondary meanings to the individual poems.

Aside from a single Latin expression, *ab aeterno* (31), in the sonnet, "A la concepción de María santísima", there is only one other poem which uses an abundance of Latinisms. This is the "Salve glosada para la natividad de María santísima" (16-17). It uses not only Latin words, but complete phrases in the language. Although it appears in four manuscripts—MSS. Duke, Madrid, Molíns, and Lima-A—it is not characteristic of Caviedes' production. It is impossible to say for certain whether the work is Caviedes' or not, but general stylistic features, including the irregularities of the form, would lead one to be skeptical of accepting it without reservations. In the following short quotation from the poem, one can easily see the excessive use of Latin words and phraseology, which have been placed in italics:

> Oy que *ad te clamamus*
> todos los miserables,
> *exules filii Evae*,
> como a Reyna triunfante,
> del común yerro y fatal ultraje;
> pues *ad te suspiramus*
> con ánimas insaciables
> ya *gementes et flentes*
> *in lacrimarun valle*. (16)

It is immediately noticeable from this short passage alone that the poem is totally unlike any other work written by Caviedes.

One of the most conspicuous baroque features of these poems is the use of *cultismos*. Although not used excessively, they are more obvious in some poems than in others. *Palabras cultas* such as *diamantino, aurora, gemir, cándido, nítido, pulquérrima, cristal, piélago, infausto, púrpura, luminosa, opaca, oculto,* and *Cupido,* among others, are most evident in the "Romance a Jesucristo" (1-8) and the "Letanías de dos esdrújulas a María santísima" (8-10).[2] The use of these and other *cultismos* serves to give the individual poems more of an aura of elegance than has been seen previously in Caviedes' poetic production.

Some of the imagery in the poems cited above is typical of the often garish ostentations of baroque works. One sees such images as "globo diamantino", "máquina errante de/luceros cristalinos", "clásica luna pulquérrima", "fuente clarísima", "líquido de cristal", and "púrpura rosa castísima" (2 and 9). Many of these images have *palabras cultas* in them and all are strikingly conspicuous.

The "Letanías de dos esdrújulas..." is probably the poem which embraces the largest number of baroque features of any single work included in this group. In order to consider it more extensively, a portion of the poem follows with subsequent observations on its baroque features:

> Tórtola que en casto tálamo,
> cándida esposa y recíproca
> víctima es al Dios Paráclito.
> Pláceme, o Aurora fúlgida,
> nítido lucero, diáfano
> clásica luna pulquérrima,
> plácido Sol sin obstáculo.
> Oyenos fuente clarísima,
> Líquido de cristal ráfago,
> piélago de aguas vivíficas,
> tácito pozo probático.
> Pláceme o Iris Pacífico,

---

[2] The vocabulary lists compiled by Dámaso Alonso in "La lengua poética de Góngora", RFE, Anejo XX (1935), 95-108, and Antonio Vilanova in "Las fuentes y los temas del 'Polifemo' de Góngora", RFE, Anejo LXVI (1957), II, 805-872, have been consulted as a basis for determining whether a word was a *cultismo* or not.

Próspero puerto a los náufragos,
áncora en fatal catástrofe,
rémora al infausto báratro. (9)

Rather than enumerate them again, attention is here called to the fact that some classical allusions and several *cultismos* are included in this short passage as are examples of rather luminous or garish imagery. The initial and final *palabras esdrújulas* are a kind of stylistic baroque *juego* in themselves. Surely they were not chosen in some cases for any other reason except that they were *esdrújulas*. Because of their excessive use, they become little more than a *juego*. The use of adjectives in initial and final positions of stress in the individual verses — "nítido lucero, diáfano", and "clásica luna pulquérrima" — places considerable emphasis on their descriptive and attributive powers, thus making them a kind of embellishment or ornamentation of the work. This hyperbolic ornamentation is further achieved through the use of superlatives. Besides the use of *pulquérrima* and *clarísima* in the last example quoted, there are several other superlatives evident in other parts of the poem—*piísimo, electísima, bellísimo, castísima* and *fortísima* (8-10).

Baroque contrasts are found in practically all of these poems. The *claro/oscuro* contrast of so many baroque works, especially in some of Góngora's poems, is found in at least one example in the "Romance a Jesucristo".

> Aurora hermosa del sol,
> que a media noche propicio
> alumbró en Belén tinieblas
> que aún duran al Judaísmo
> Preciosísimo Lucero
> a cuyos intactos giros
> no se le opone la sombra
> de la culpa a deslucirlo.
> (MS. Madrid, 136v)

In this metaphorical reference to the Virgin, the poet provides a series of light/dark contrasts, as one sees in certain words and phrases suc as "Aurora...del sol", "media noche", "alumbró", "tinieblas", "Lucero", "sombra", and "deslucirlo".

Conceptual contrasts are also used, particularly in the works in which the poet wishes to emphasize his sinfulness in contrast with God's immaculateness. In one passage alone, a portion of which follows, a consecutive series of seventeen such contrasts is used:

> Vos, el Todopoderoso,
> yo el todo pobre e inicuo.
> Vos el sumamente sabio,
> yo el sumamente imperito.
> Vos, lleno de todas ciencias
> yo de la ignorancia abismo.
> Vos, quien todo lo sujeta,
> yo el que a todo me rindo.
> ....
> Vos, noble, yo envilecido;
> Vos, el todo, yo la nada;
> Vos, la gloria, yo el conflicto... (6)

This same type of parallel contrast is used quite often in these religious poems and represents one of the stylistic features of the group (23 and 25).

Baroque antitheses are also evident in some of the poems In many cases an antithesis is used to stress the infinite greatness of God or of Heaven. Such is the case in the following tercets from the sonnet entitled "Prueba que se ve a Dios más patente, que cuando al hombre le parece que no hay Dios":

> Repare el entendido que ocultarse
> a entendimiento y vista es descubrirse,
> porque es un concederse en el negarse,
> pues si a sus perfecciones ha de unirse,
> su gobernar no es dado interpretarse,
> luego es prueba que hay Dios el encubrirse. (27)

The technique is used for the same purpose in the following quotation in which the magnificence of Heaven makes even the greatest of earthly qualities seem insignificant in contrast:

> ¡O juicios del cielo, inescrutables,
> donde el mayor saber es ignorancia,
> tan extremos, tan raros y admirables!

que está más cerca la mayor distancia,
alentáos, pecadores miserables,
que mucho pierden para más ganancia. (25)

Many other techniques besides those which are obviously baroque are worthy of note. The elaborate metaphors used to refer to God, Christ, and the Virgin total over eighty in number by themselves alone. Most of the metaphors for God are not based on visual or other sensory imagery, but on concepts. Many refer to qualities that are part of God's many attributes, as one sees in some of the following metaphors: "Sumo Saber" (28), "el Poderoso" (27), "el sabio" (27), "el prudente" (27), "el portentoso" (27), "el grande" (27), "Dueño del alma" (23), "Padre Amado" (24), "Padre piísimo" (8), "Sabio unigénito" (8), and "Hacedor" (97). One metaphor, "Pelícano divino" (22), because of its rarity is worthy of special note. In the poem in which it is found, the author speaks of the Sacred Host and the fact that it is the flesh and blood of God. The reference to God as "Pelícano" alludes to the unfounded but common folkloristic belief that the pelican opened its own breast to feed its young with its blood. The poet thus suggests that in this case God feeds his children on his flesh and blood in the Sacrament.

The metaphors for Christ are less numerous with the major portion of them being easily understood. He is called, among other things, "Crucificado Cordero" (1), "Monarca" (3), "Redentor mío" (13), "Redentor del Universo" (14), "Hijo soberano" (10), and "Hijo sagrado" (11).

The most elaborate system of metaphors is that which refers to the Virgin. Although many of them are easily understood, others are farther removed in significance and their meanings are somewhat obscured, as can be seen in the following series: "la que culpa original no tuvo" (4), "Abogada Nuestra" (MS. Madrid, 136v), "Aurora hermosa del sol" (MS. Madrid, 136v), "Preciosísimo Lucero" (MS. Madrid, 137v), "tu soberana madre [de Jesús]" (14), "mi protectora [del poeta]" (14), "Hija electísima" (9), "Puérpera del Padre oráculo" (9), "Paloma humílima" (9), "Tórtola" (9), "Cándida esposa" (9), "Aurora fúlgida" (9), "Iris Pacífico" (9), "áncora en fatal catástrofe" (9), "rémora al infausto báratro" (9), "púrpura rosa castísima" (9), "Judit fortísima" (9), "ínclita belona" (9), "bélica Jael" (9), "máxima Palas" (9), and "Ester benéfica" (9).

In other metaphors sinners are referred to as "el inmundo" (27), "el soez" (27), "el asqueroso" (27), and "el incapaz" (27); the Archangel is the "Soberano Virrey de aquel Señor" (30); and Lucifer is the "dragón soberbio e infernal" (30).

As has been seen in the preceding paragraphs, the variety of metaphorical allusions, especially to people, is quite extensive and elaborate. Only those to medical men, as seen in the poetry of social satire, are in any way comparable in scope to the ones used in this poetry of a religious nature.

Attention has already been called to the use of chromatic and other visual imagery in the discussion of baroque features of these poems. One should not be led to believe, however, that such visual imagery is the only kind used. In the following verses from a sonnet, one can see how subtle *matices* are mixed with metallic colors:

> Lutos de humo el fuego macilentan,
> ....
> Cambia su oro el sol en cobre aciago,
> la plata de la luna se convierte
> en el plomo que admira el Areópago. (26)

As might be expected in this poetry of a religious nature, some of the visual imagery is not at all different from that commonly found in works of this type. Images of Christ dwell especially on his suffering during the time of the Crucifixion, as one sees in the following examples: "vos muerto" (1), "vos atado" (1), "vuestro rostro herido" (1), "vos azotado" (2), "un cuerpo lastimado" (3), "tu corona de espinas" (14), and "el sagrado madero/ de la cruz en que moriste" (14).

Auditory and olfactory imagery is found in greater abundance in this group of poems than in any other yet studied. In the sonnet entitled "Al conmoverse la naturaleza en la muerte de Christo", the poet uses a series of auditory images to show how Nature reacted at the moment when Christ died.

> Muere el Author, sus obras se lamentan,
> suspira el viento en recios ventarrones,

gime la tierra, tiembla exhalaciones,
llora el agua, por fuentes que revientan.
... ...
borrascas brama el mar con los tritones,
perece el cielo haciendo admiraciones,
cruje el eje, los polos se violentan. (26)

In the following four verses one finds examples of olfactory images which are in reality metaphorical references to the Virgin:

Oyenos, mirra odorífica
semilla al fragante bálsamo,
púrpura rosa castísima,
cándido lirio aromático. (9)

In these examples of sensorial imagery, the characteristic which is noted first and foremost is that the images are refined and cultured. In some cases they are totally unlike those of the poet in the satirical works.

Because many of these works are of a meditative nature and have little to do with earthly or physical things, there are many poems which are abstract and conceptual and have little sensorial imagery. In the initial quatrains of the sonnet entitled "Para saber el enojo de Dios", one sees that the primary emphasis is placed on concepts and not on the senses:

Para saber que a Dios tengo enojado
y tener de su ira cierta ciencia,
examen haz de hacer de tu conciencia
e igual será tu enojo a tu pecado.
Con aquesto tendrás averiguado
cómo estará, sin otra diligencia,
porque la culpa es signo de evidencia
que por aquesta a Dios tienes airado. (30)

Among the other techniques commonly utilized by Caviedes in his poetic art is the parallel construction. Its most common purpose in these specific works is to bring out and develop a long series of contrasts, as has already been noted on other occasions. The sonnet "Al conocimiento de Dios y la criatura" has parallel contrasting constructions in the initial quatrains, which are stylistically much like those of the "Romance a Jesucristo"

(6). In these eight verses one sees how Caviedes used the technique to emphasize and even exaggerate God's infinite qualities in opposition to his own sinful state:

> Yo la más vil criatura de la tierra,
> Vos, el grande, el Señor, el Poderoso,
> yo el inmundo, el soez, el asqueroso,
> Vos aquel en quien todo bien se encierra.
> Yo el incapaz que ciego siempre yerra,
> Vos el sabio, el prudente, el portentoso,
> yo el pecador injusto, al cielo odioso,
> Vos, quien del, por mis culpas me destierra. (27).

In the second of the two poems mentioned above, the *romance*, the structure of the parallelism is at first the same as that of the sonnet, but as the intensity of the parallel enumerations grows, the constructions become shorter, as one sees in the following example of the technique:

> Vos, el sosiego, yo el pleito;
> Vos, el triunfo, yo el vencido;
> Vos, el fuerte, el flaco yo;
> Vos, la razón, yo el delirio;
> Vos, la gracia, yo la culpa,
> y, en fin, para abreviar, digo:
> que en criatura y criador
> hay un extremo infinito. (6)

One can see here quite clearly the parallelism of dominant words and expressions in each of the initial verses.

Another technique which has not been found often in this study of Caviedes' works is the use of oxymoron. It is not surprising to find it used in these poems, however, since it has already been observed that antitheses and contrasts are prevalent. In the following four verses the statement has two seemingly contradictory components, since silence usually does not serve to explain anything:

> tengan lo no exagerado
> por lo más encarecido,
> pues donde la voz no alcanza
> ¡con el silencio lo explico! (4)

The musicality of many of the sound patterns in these works is augmented by the use of alliteration. Although a few cases of this technique have been noted before, they have never been quite so abundant as they are in the following examples: "Crucificado Cordero/cuyo poder infinito" (1), "tantas tormentas tranquilas" (MS. Madrid, 136v), "Señor, muerto/y yo mirándoos muerto tengo vida" (23), and "que pudieran/decir que la consorte os costó cara" (24).

Internal rhyme is also used to achieve comparable musical effects and sound patterns in some poems. The poet says: "tengo un Dios como Vos" (24), "Cuidado con tus potencias/y sentidos ten, atento" (18), and finally one sees "adorarte, alabarte, amarte y verte" (22).

The use of apostrophe is another feature found in this religious poetry. In some cases the poet addresses Nature's phenomena as though they were alive: "¡cielos!, ¿estábais dormidos?" and "Elementos, ¿para cuándo/guardábais los torbellinos...?" (2). A related technique, personification, is used in the sonnet "Al conmoverse la naturaleza en la muerte de Christo" (26), in which *viento, tierra, agua, mar, cielo, eje,* and *polos* all take on human qualities and vociferate their grief at the time of the Crucifixion. In yet another poem the author's heart is personified, as is seen in the verses "a Ti corazón se postra humilde,/porque de contemplarte desfallece" (22). Personification in these works is used principally to activate and make a situation come alive with movement at a time when little is expected.

Insofar as lexicon is concerned, several observations have already been made regarding its baroque features. The large number of *cultismos* is the most salient of these lexical features. Another element which stands out is the startling number of *palabras esdrújulas*, one hundred ten of them, found in a single poem (8-10). Unlike the other groups of poems, not a single Americanism has been noted in any of these thirty-two works. Latinisms, except for those in the "Salve glosada para la natividad de María santísima" (16-17), are practically non-existent. The language of these works could best be described as cultured and refined in direct contrast to the less sophisticated and often regional vocabulary of the poetry of social satire.

The most noteworthy syntactical feature of this group of poems is the abundance of modifying adjectives for a single noun. At times they might almost be compared to the architectural filigree of a baroque church. Innumerable examples of three or more post-positioned adjectives are to be found throughout these works, as one sees in the following examples:

> Congojado mi espíritu cobarde,
> vergonzoso y confuso, llega a veros... (24)

> ...siendo
> un Dios los tres en esencia
> poderoso, fuerte, inmenso. (15)

> ni cielo puede haber sin esta estrella,
> que es más clara, lucida y más hermosa... (26)

> sino un solo Dios eterno
> inmenso, increado y santo. (10)

> ¡O juicios del Cielo, inescrutables
> donde el mayor saber es ignorancia
> tan extremos, tan raros y admirables! (25)

The same technique of multiple adjectival modifiers for a single noun is used for ante-positioned adjectives, as illustrated by the following:

> ¿no se tronchó en sus lucientes,
> constantes, eternos quicios? (2)

> ofensas contra el inmenso,
> perfecto, eterno y amable
> Redentor del Universo... (13-14)

One work, the "Letanías de dos esdrújulas...", already cited on several occasions, stands forth from all others in its use of both attributive and descriptive adjectives. In the following short quotation from the poem, one can see the abundance of adjectives, which are in italics, in each verse:

> Pláceme, ciprés *bellísimo*
> símbolo al *fecundo* plátano,

mística zarza que *ignífera*
óptima es e *ileso* sándalo.
Óyenos, mirra *odorífica*
semilla al *fragante* bálsamo,
púrpura rosa *castísima,*
cándido lirio *aromático,*
pláceme, Judit *fortísima,*
ínclita Belona en ánimo,
bélica Jael al Sísara,
máxima Palas al tártaro. (9)

This particular poem has a wide variety of adjectives throughout the work. Although it represents one extreme of their use, Caviedes does use considerably more adjectives in this group of poems than have been noted in any other that has been considered thus far.

It has been observed in this portion of the study of Caviedes' works that his religious poetry forms a distinct and at times contrasting aspect when compared with the sections already studied. The religious themes and subject matter together with the lyric expression of the poet are presented in predominantly Italianate meters with the sonnet being the form which is most commonly used.

The poems' most salient features of baroque epoch style are seen in the use of *cultismos,* allusions, a few Latinisms, and above all the antitheses and contrasts. *Cultismos* and chromatic lexicon provide some rather garish imagery which is quite typical of many baroque works of the epoch. There is also some evidence of a stylistic *juego,* but *conceptismo* and *juegos de palabras* are not noted extensively in these works.

Metaphorical expressions are found predominantly in the references to God, Christ, and the Virgin for whom some eighty different metaphors are used. Most of the imagery is visual, although several examples of olfactory and auditory imagery are to be encountered. Among the rhetorical figures most employed by the poet are parallelisms, enumerations, oxymoron, alliteration, internal rhyme, apostrophe, and personification which are all to be noted in varying degrees of frequency.

In the lexical elements considered, attention has been called to the use of *palabras cultas* and a large number of *esdrújulos* which are found in some of the individual works. Americanisms are noteworthy only because of their absence. The overabundance of both attributive and descriptive adjectives in some poems represents at least one distinguishable syntactical feature of Caviedes' particular style.

The poems which have been studied in this chapter represent yet another facet of Caviedes' art. As in the case of the amorous poetry, the importance of these works has been diminished somewhat by the greater popularity of the satirical poems. They are not as good in all their multiple aspects as the latter, but some of the individual works, which have been considered here, cannot be eclipsed by even the best of the satires. Probably the most aesthetically appealing features are those found in baroque elements of style and technique and in the fervent sincerity with which the poet addresses God, Christ, and the Virgin. It might be said that these works make up the post-apex of Caviedes' entire poetic production, since they would most logically correspond to the time when the poet was older, more meditative, and more conscious of the needs of his immortal soul.

Chapter VII

MISCELLANEOUS POEMS

The poems which will be considered in this final group are those which do not seem to fit, by reason of theme or subject, into any of the other divisions of the author's works. Some of the poems within this miscellaneous group show similarities of subject matter among themselves, but the small number in each subdivision would make it unwise to devote an entire chapter to them, since not more than three to eight poems can be grouped together in any one instance. The seventy poems which are included in this group deal with death, riches and poverty, contemporary subjects, Nature's phenomena, as well as others which meditate on the significance of life. Classical themes are also found in three different poems. Three other works which do not seem to fit into any of these subjects are the "Defensa de un pedo" (*Doc.*, 109-112), the "Carta que escribió el autor a la monja de México, habiéndole ésta enviado a pedir algunas obras de sus versos, siendo ella en esto y en todo el mayor ingenio de estos siglos" (32-36), and the "Coloquio entre la vieja y Periquillo sobre una procesión en Lima" (83-93). The remainder, and largest portion, of this miscellaneous grouping is made up of forty *agudas* and *epigramas,* which are short poems on a wide variety of subjects.

Several different situations are presented in these poems, although it should be noted that situation is generally not so important as it is, for example, in some of the poetry of social satire. In the works which deal with death, the poet dwells on the passing of several different people. In one of these, "A la muerte de mi esposa" (78), the author laments the loss of his wife. In others he writes about the death of Melchor de Navarra y RocaFull, Duque de la Palata and twenty-second viceroy of Peru (105-106). Since it is known that the Duque de la Palata died in Portobelo, Panama, on April 13, 1691, as he was returning to Spain, it is possible to place this poem chronologically among the later works produced by Caviedes, although certainly not his last. In the *romance* entitled "A mi muerte próxima" (295), the poet presents his personal attitudes toward his own approaching death. Stylistically this poem is not unlike Caviedes' other works, but it does not appear in any of the known manuscripts. It is found in both the Odriozola and Palma editions, but their sources for this particular work are not mentioned by either of the respective editors.

Another subject celebrated in three different sonnets (102-103) is the construction of the first permanent dock at Callao whose port was of vital importance to the city of Lima. The actual building of the dock was brought about under the direction of the Conde de la Monclova, another Peruvian viceroy, and the work was completed in 1696.[1] Of all Caviedes' works these are the latest poems which can be chronologically dated. Another contemporary occurrence, which is the subject and basic situation for two poems (79-83 and 95), is the earthquake which utterly destroyed Lima in 1687. In these two works the poet vividly describes the horrors brought about by this cataclysm.

Three other poems present mythological situations. In them the poet describes respectively the myths of Narcissus and Echo (197-201), Jupiter and Io (147-153), and the fable of Polyphemus and Galatea in which even Ulysses appears (117-129). Although the latter is somewhat reminiscent of Góngora's "La fábula de Polifemo y Galatea," the comparison can not be aptly drawn on any elements other than subject matter, as a perusal of both works easily shows.[2]

---

[1] Manuel de Mendiburu, *Diccionario histórico-biográfico del Perú* (Lima, 1885), VI, 540.

[2] See Dámaso Alonso, *Góngora y el 'Polifemo'* (Madrid, 1960). This edition includes the text of the poem, a version in prose, commentaries, and notes by this outstanding Spanish critic.

The characters presented in these different situations are quite diverse. Actual persons who were contemporaries of Caviedes include his wife (78), the Duque de la Palata (105-106), the Conde de la Monclova (102), and Sor Juana Inés de la Cruz (32-36). Another real person mentioned is the Maestro Baes who was an important theologian and teacher in Lima during the late sixteenth century.[3] Mythological characters include Narcissus, Echo, Jupiter, Io, Argus, Polyphemus, Galatea, and Assis (197-201, 147-153, and 117-129). The only other fictional characters of import are Periquillo and a *vieja* who appear in the "Coloquio entre la vieja y Periquillo sobre una procesión en Lima" (83-93). Aside from these actual persons and fictional characters mentioned here, there are no others of any great importance.

The point of view of these works reveals some interesting ideas on their essential nature as a group. Forty of them are narrated in the third person and are either descriptive or informative in nature. This is in direct contrast to the other facets of the poet's works in which either the lyric *yo* predominates, or the work is addressed in the second person singular to a specific person. Only seven of these poems are completely lyric with the remainder being addressed to specific or indefinite persons in *tú*. It might be noted, however, that the *agudas* and *epigramas* account for a large number of the poems which are narrated exclusively in the third person.

Death is the theme which is most commonly found in these particular poems. This is quite evident in the works dealing with the demise of the author's wife (78), the Duque de la Palata (105-106), Maestro Baes (58-60), and of the poet's own approaching death (295). In one of the sonnets, Caviedes gives his own definitions of what death is, as one sees in the following:

> La muerte viene a ser cumplirse un plazo,
> un saber lo que el hombre en vida ignora,
> un instante postrero de la hora,
> susurro que al tocarla deja el mazo,
> último aprieto con que estrecha el lazo,

---

[3] Luis Antonio Eguiguren, *Catálogo histórico del claustro de la Universidad de San Marcos (1576-1800)* (Lima, 1912), p. 60.

> la ejecución mortal por pecadora,
> un pesar que el ageno siente y llora,
> un descuido que al vivo da embarazo,
> eterno enigma es, pues nadie sabe
> cómo es la muerte, quando está viviendo,
> ni, en finando, si queda luego iluso
> y así tan solo el punto en que se acaba
> nuestra vida, se sabe a lo que entiendo,
> con que el temerla no es razón, sino uso. (95).

Love is a secondary theme which appears in two of the poems that are based on mythological subject matter (147-153 and 117-129). It should be noted, however, that this theme does not predominate in a large number of poems and is not so ostensible a theme as is death.

Several different theses can be extracted from these works. On the subject of riches and poverty, one finds such theses as "Throw away your money and you will be happy" (204), "Wealth is the enemy of happiness in life" (98), "A poor man will become even poorer" (98), "Wealth only turns to dust with the passage of time" (98-99), "Be an unscrupulous person and you will become rich" (98-99), and "People usually get rich by lying, cheating, and stealing" (107-108). In the poems which deal with earthquakes and comets, the author states that "Earthquakes are not God's punishment for the sinful, since they occur whether one sins or not" (108), and "Comets are natural phenomena and are not omens of doom" (190-191).[4] In his advice for judges one finds the thesis that "He who will judge others must first learn to judge himself" (101). In general advice on life, the poet suggests that "Knowledge and reason give the greatest happiness in life" (110). In yet another poem Caviedes states that "Everything in life is uncertain and illusory", as one sees in the following sonnet:

> Todo el mundo se funda en opiniones
> y en realidades no, porque juzgamos
> contrarios, en aquello que tocamos,

---

[4] The thesis of these two poems is the same as that of Carlos de Sigüenza y Góngora, the Mexican savant, who in a sustained *pleito* with the Jesuit Eusebio Francisco Kino likewise asserted that comets were natural phenomena and not omens of doom. It is somewhat surprising that a man of Caviedes'

en parecer, en obras y en acciones.
Todas son conjeturas e ilusiones,
porque siempre lo cierto adivinamos,
todos en duda la verdad hallamos,
envuelta con mentiras y ficciones,
certeza alguna en nada nos tenemos,
si todo es conjetura, todo indicio
de un saber presumir si no sabemos,
de lo que hay que saber ni aun un resquicio,
pues a juzgar de cierto lo que vemos
nada habrá que admirar en el juicio. (99)

The large number of theses in these works, when compared with those already discussed, is due primarily, it would seem, to the informative and didactic nature of many of the poems. As noted previously, over half of them are narrated in the third person and present ideas on a wide variety of subjects.

There are no forms in this group of poems which do not appear with varying degrees of frequency in some of the other facets of the author's works. The sonnet, which is used twenty-one times, predominates over all other forms. All but two of these sonnets have a classical rhyme; the two exceptions have a rhyme scheme of ABBA:ABBA in the quatrains and CDE:CDE in the tercets. Only one other sonnet of this type appears in all of Caviedes' works. The remainder of the poems consists of twelve *romances*, a single *endecha real*, a poem of *cuartetas* and another of *redondillas*. Apart from these more highly structured forms, single *cuartetas*, *redondillas*, and *quintillas* make up the forty *agudas* and *epigramas* contained in the occasional verse. None of these forms is really atypical of Caviedes' art, since they all appear with varying degrees of frequency in the other facets of the poet's works which have already been analyzed and described. The predominance of the sonnet over other forms does substantiate the fact that a large number of these works deal with refined subject matter, as opposed to the popular subject matter of the poetry of social satire, for example, in which traditional forms such as the *romance* are most

---

limited education should show such maturity of thought in an epoch when superstition still reigned supreme. See Carlos de Sigüenza y Góngora, *Libra astronómica y filosófica*, ed. Bernabé Navarro (Mexico, 1959).

commonly encountered. Aside from these comments on form, it may also be noted that there are no evident metrical innovations which might serve to distinguish these works from any others written during that epoch.

One technique of internal structure, which is used in two of these poems, is the epistolary form. In the "Carta que escribió el autor a la monja de México..." (32-36), the entire *romance* is a letter addressed to Sor Juana Inés de la Cruz. The poet begins the letter as follows and respectfully addresses her as *vos:*

> Por vuestro ingenio divino,
> sutil, la del oro llaman,
> si a influjos los dos de Apolo
> cultiváis venas de Arabia,
> el aplauso vuestro es tal
> que porque sabio sonara,
> en docto clarín de letras
> fundió de bronce la fama... (32)

Caviedes continues praising Sor Juana's art as a poetess and adds a few autobiographical facts about himself. Before closing the letter, he also mentions that he is sending her some of his own works, since the *monja mexicana* had previously written him asking for them. Unfortunately Sor Juana's letter to the poet has not been encountered to the present.

In the *romance* entitled "Polifemo y Galatea", the epistolary technique is again used, but it does not comprise the entire poem, as was the case of the previously cited work. In it Polyphemus writes to Galatea to accuse her of being unfaithful to him.

> "Trinchitaria Galatea,
> que viene a ser siete grados
> más que ramera, ya he visto
> tu amor y tu aleve trato.
> Bien sé que a otro pastor quieres
> porque te guarde el ganado
> cabrío, que estás haciendo,
> pero no he de ser yo el manso;
> . . . .
> Quédate para quien eres
> y quieres al pastor villano

muchos años. Y los dioses
te guarden mientras te mato.
Polifemo." (124)

As can readily be seen, Polyphemus admonishes Galatea for not being true to him and for falling in love with another. He even threatens to kill her if she does not heed his warnings. The epistolary form is used here primarily as a means of filling in knowledge of actions which have not been specifically treated prior to this point. From what has been seen in this example, one might say that it is essentially a technique utilized for exposition.

Among other techniques that are used for internal development in some of these poems, one finds the rhetorical question. In the *romance* "A la muerte del Maestro Baes", rhetorical questions are used in the initial verses of the poem as a means of building up an immediate intensity or suspense in the work. The technique in this case is technically known as anacoenosis, since no answer will be forthcoming. This is quite apparent since the poet directs himself in an apostrophe to *cielos, mares, tierra, estrellas,* and *luceros*— things that would not logically answer unless completely personified.

Cielos, mares, tierra
¿cómo insensibles e inmobles
estáis? ¡o no ha muerto Baes
o sois, sin duda, de bronce!
¿Cómo no lloráis estrellas,
pálidas constelaciones,
dando en fúnebres cometas
lágrimas de fuego al orbe?
¿Cómo no apagáis, luceros
los diamantinos blandones,
para que ahumando pavesas
copos vistáis a los montes? (58)

The use of the rhetorical question in yet another poem appears as anthypophora, since an answer is provided to the interrogatives. The questions are addressed in an apostrophe to Lima, but it is not the city that responds. Instead, the poet answers the questions for Lima.

¿Qué se hicieron, Lima ilustre,
tus fuertes arquitecturas
de templos, casas y torres,
como la fama divulga?
¿Dónde están los altosanos,
cincelados de molduras,
portadas, bóvedas, arcos,
pilastras, jaspes, columnas?
Mas responderás que todo
lo han derribado las culpas,
que en temblores disfrazadas
contra el hombre se conjuran. (82)

In this specific example the technique is used to point out and emphasize the fallacious belief of the people of the time that earthquakes were God's means of punishing sinners. Lima is not just the city alone in this poem, but is actually all of the people who form a part of the city.

One other poem is worthy of special mention at this point. Reference is made to the "Coloquio entre la vieja y Periquillo sobre una procesión celebrada en Lima" (83-93). It is most significant because of its drama-like structure. The entire poem consists of a dialogue between the *vieja* and Periquillo with a short narrated introduction, which is somewhat comparable to the description of a scene at the beginning of a play. In this respect it is much like Caviedes' three *bayles*, which were his only dramatic productions. The main differences are, however, that only two characters are involved and emphasis is placed on the substance of the dialogue and not on action.

La anciana curiosidad
frágil, femenil dolencia,
total, prolijo cuidado
de las sucesoras de Eva,
pregunta al niño de Guacos,
bobo de Coria en simpleza,
hijo de madre arrullona,
nene por niño de teta,
Perico es de estos palotes
y aunque periquitos le echan,
cuenta todo de pe a pa,
al pie de su inculta letra.
... ...

Vieja	Contadme, niño, contadme, sin que la pasión te mueva, sus progresos, sus trofeos, sus máquinas, sus grandezas.
Per.	Abuelita mía, yo aunque contártelo quiera, no estoy muy al cabo y temo de darte muy malas nuevas, demás que yo, divertido con los niños de la escuela, juega jugando, vi sólo unas niñerías meras.
Vieja	Decidlas, niño, decidlas no te hagas tan de nuevas, que los melindres enfadan, por ser, niño, cosa vieja. (83-84)

Many salient features of baroque epoch style are evident in these poems, although not to such a degree as either the strong influence of *conceptismo* in the poetry of social satire or that of *culteranismo* in the religious works. In the poems included in this group, a few examples of *conceptismo* are found. In the "Juicio del cometa", one sees some play on the concept of the words *cola* and *rabo*:

>   Con la cola vaticinan,
>   y discurren con acierto,
>   porque con cola se pueden
>   pegar los chascos al pueblo.
>   ... ...
>   No son pecados veniales
>   los que se mienten en esto
>   pues son pecados con rabo,
>   porque en cola están mintiendo. (190)

In a subsequent portion of the same poem, there is a conceptual pun and contrast on the words *corba, corcobados,* and *derechos:*

>   Con tener corba la espalda [el cometa]
>   anuncia que habrá estupendos
>   corcobados, aunque no
>   son vaticinios derechos. (191)

The "Fábula burlesca de Júpiter e Io" contains another example of *conceptismo*. The key to the conceit involves the knowledge of the fact that Jupiter turned Io, the *Ninfa* mentioned in the following example, into a cow:

> Ablandóse, pues, la Ninfa,
> porque entonces era blanda,
> si de por fuerza es ternera
> la que ha de volverse vaca. (149)

In the *romance* entitled "Narciso y Eco" one finds also a *juego de palabras* which is centered around the words *carabana* and *cara vana*:

> No era muy estraña aquesta
> en las que son cortesanas,
> pues mil carabanas tiene
> y esta es una cara vana. (199)

Another baroque characteristic that is noted at times in these works is excessive exaggeration. Perhaps the most evident example of hyperbole is found in the description of the giant Polyphemus in the *romance* entitled "Polifemo y Galatea" (117-129). The description of the giant actually involves some forty-eight verses of which only a portion are quoted in the following:

> Medíase con el cielo
> o poquito más abajo,
> mil leguas, porque no digan
> que yo le quito o añado.
> ... ...
> La nariz era disforme,
> pues, además de lo largo,
> eran las ventanas puertas
> y el caballete caballo.
> Era la boca una gruta,
> los dientes eran peñascos,
> la barba era de ballena,
> y el pescuezo un campanario.
> Por hombros tenía las
> Peñas de Francia y de Martos,
> los brazos eran de mar,
> siendo dos remos las manos.
> Un cable de Capitana
> con dos anclas en los cabos

ceñía por cinto, y
le abrochaba reventando. (117-118)

Bright, garish imagery of the type often found in many baroque works is evident in some of these poems. In one of the sonnets written at the time of the completion of the dock at el Callao, this type of imagery is quite ostensible, as illustrated by the following:

> Recién nacido escollo, a quien veneran
> las ondas que tu pie besan errantes,
> salpicándote el pecho de diamantes
> las que sin dar el choque vidrios eran.
> En cuidado tan grande no se vieran
> sus olas de zafiros inconstantes,
> si tus piedras sus aguas incesantes
> argentadas a golpes no volvieran.
> Si de la espuma naces procelosa,
> eres nevado y claro descendiente
> de Venus bella, cristalina diosa,
> y siendo parto suyo, es consecuente
> ser engendro tu fábrica famosa
> de Monclova, que es Marte en lo valiente. (103)

One also notes in this same poem the classical allusions to Venus and Mars.

The same type of ostentatious, luminous imagery is seen in the sonnet "Al terremoto que asoló esta ciudad", especially in its initial quatrains:

> Quando el alba, que es prólogo del día,
> el blandor de los orbes avivaba
> en doradas cenizas, que alentaba
> del fénix de la luz que renacía,
> segoviana ostentaba argentería
> la luna que de plata se llenaba
> a cuyo cetro el aire se alteraba
> que la tierra en cavernas suprimía. (95)

Besides the mythological characters found in some of the poems, there are numerous classical allusions in them and other works. The poet mentions, among others, Phoebus (78 and 58), Diana (58), Phaëthon (59), Cepheus (59), Achilles (59), Hector

(59), Apollo (59), Orpheus (59), Theseus (60), Neptune (102), Venus (103), Mars (103), Icarus (58 and 95), Juno (149), Argus (150), and Mercury (151). In most cases the poet alludes to these mythological figures as a means of evoking some prowess, deed, or attribute, which they performed or had, that can give additional significance and secondary meaning to a situation created by the author.

As is usually the case in Caviedes' works, the Latinisms which appear are mostly simple clichés which are used on occasion. Words and phrases such as *Quia ventus et vita mea* (*Doc.*, 112), *avis rara* (295), *nemini parco* (60), *non plus* (120), *maremagnum* (83), and *in voce* (88) are not examples which would demand a thorough knowledge of Latin on the part of the poet in order to employ them accurately in his works. They do not seem to serve any particular aesthetic purpose, but do add somewhat to the complexity of the works.

One final feature of baroque style, which is found repeatedly in these works, is the use of hyperbaton. In many of the cases this involves the unnatural separation of a noun from its modifying adjectives by one or more lexical elements, as in the following: "un bocado de riscos poderoso" (103), "no veneran/humana ya criatura" (82), "segoviana ostentaba argentería/la luna" (95), "y es cierto, si andan los rabos/con cosas malas revueltos" (190), and "Alimentos dais de versos/a cuantos de hacerlos tratan/hermanos" (35). In other cases hyperbaton is found in complexities of word order, as in the following citation:

> Eco por nombre tenía
> una ninfa, que habitaba
> a la falda de los montes,
> que son quien la voz rechaza. (197)

Perhaps a more logical prose rendition of the verses above would be, "Una ninfa, que habitaba a la falda de los montes que son quien la voz rechaza, tenía por nombre Eco". Such complexities of word order can be explained at times through impositions of meter and rhyme, but in this and many other cases, it is obviously an intentional use of hyperbaton.

It should be noted in these observations on the salient features of epoch style that not every poem in this group has such baroque features or at least the characteristics are not so apparent. Since the works are possibly from different periods of development in the poet's art, they are not at all consistent in their multiple stylistic features.

Among the other techniques and figures used by Caviedes in his poetic art, one finds a paucity of metaphors. The poet refers to his wife as "mi sol" (78); the sky is "azul bóveda" (59); the dock at Callao is a "dura mordaza de labradas rocas" and "recién nacido escollo" (102-103); the heavens are "celestes estancias" (149); Jupiter is "el tronera mayor" (149); the dawn is "la Aurora" (151); Argus' eyes are "oculares ventanas" (151); and Sor Juana Inés de la Cruz is referred to as an "amazona de discretos" (35) and "beldad discreta" (35). None of these metaphors distinguishes itself to any extent, nor is any so rare that the original meaning is lost or difficult to understand.

In the remarks on baroque features, evidence of the luminous and garish imagery employed in some of the poems has already been noted. This same type of imagery is combined in the "Fábula de Júpiter e Io" with images of instruments of war. Such imagery has already been noted in other portions of Caviedes' works. In this particular poem luminous and garish images together with those of war instruments are employed primarily in a description of the nymph Io, as one sees in the following exerpts from the poem:

> Érase una ninfa hermosa,
> muy pálida y muy peinada
> que otro tanto que éste fue
> un hombre de mucha gala.
> Cera blanca y pelinegra,
> para ser más agraciada,
> que morena y pelirubia
> no vale lo que una blanca. [5]
> ... ...

---

[5] One can also note the baroque contrasts in the initial verses, *cera blanca/pelinegra* and *morena/pelirubia*. Besides the contrasts in the individual verses, there is also a parallel contrast between *blanca/morena* and *pelinegra/*

> Tenía en las cejas dos
> escopetas apuntadas,
> que el matar con flechas y arcos
> es muerte de coplas rancias.
> Salgamos ya de un Amor
> con arco, harpones y aljabas
> y tengamos un Cupido
> con mosquete y bala rasa.
> ... ...
> Era un carámbano terso
> que por las cejas colgaba
> de la nieve derretida,
> de la frente tersa y clara,
> que a dividir las mejillas
> bajó un arroyo de plata,
> floreciendo en su frescura
> dos primaveras de nácar. (147-148)

Auditory images are also used in some of these works. In the first of these examples, "Suspire el Cephiro manso,/gima uracanes el Norte" (59), one hears the sounds of Nature. In yet another poem Caviedes tries to convey some of the ominous sounds heard when the earthquake struck Lima.

> Precipitadas las cumbres
> con ronco estruendo se asustan;
> los valles a roncos ecos
> trájicamente retumban. (80)

Many of the other techniques employed in these poems have already been noted as integral parts of the author's art in his other works. One of these is the use of parallel constructions. In the example which follows, the technique is used for its repetitive nature which gives emphasis to what the poet is saying: "¡Me moriré! buen provecho./¡Me moriré! en hora buena..." (295), while in another case the construction presents parallelism of meaning as well as dominant words.

---

pelirubia. Finally, there is also an element of *conceptismo* in the phrase "no vale una blanca" in which the word *blanca* has the double meaning of white and the small monetary unit.

> Horrores copia la noche,
> terrores pinta la pluma,
> lástimas dibuja el genio
> a las edades futuras. (79)

Parallelism is not limited to just dominant words in successive verses alone, but in some cases it involves complete constructions. This is specially true of the poems in which rhetorical questions are used, since most of the questions make up a series of four successive verses (58 and 82).

The use of enumerations has also been noted in the analysis of Caviedes' other works. In some instances these enumerations are also parallel as in the final phrases of the following quotation:

> ¿Luego todas las plausibles
> pompas que el mundo celebra
> de esa confusa Babel,
> de esa fabulosa Creta,
> de esa imaginaria Menfis,
> de esa fantástica Atenas...? (92)

The same technique is evident again in another example taken from the same work:

> todo paja, nada grano,
> cascos vanos, tripas huecas,
> mucho ruido, pocas nueces,
> muchos dones, pocas rentas. (92)

These enumerations are usually employed, it would seem, as a means of emphasizing and intensifying the importance of something that is being said.

One case of personification is found in Caviedes' *romance* "Al terremoto acaecido en Lima..." In this work the mountains seem to take on life when the poet says:

> cuando, blandiéndose el orbe,
> los montes se descoyuntan,
> abriendo bocas que horribles
> braman por las espeluncas. (79-80)

Alliteration is often employed by the poet in a variety of situations. Whether the technique is intentional or not is of course uncertain, but it does seem to add to the over-all poetic and musical effect of the poems in which it is used. In the following example the initial letter "s" is repeated seven times:

> Que solo sé que no sé,
> y aún si el no saber supiera,
> ya eso fuera saber algo
> y eso mi ignorancia niega. (92)

In other poems the alliteration is not so pronounced, as in the following examples in which the initial letter "p" is repeated: "y estando en el agua nunca/pudo el pobre pescarla" (198) and "copiarlo en embrión pretendo/porque no hay para pintarlo/de todo punto pincel" (117).

Internal rhyme is found only a few isolated examples. One sees some evidence of the technique in "Bola es el mundo que sola..." (203) and "el gozo en el pozo era..." (198). It is not a technique which appears often in these works, nor was it extremely noticeable in those already examined.

Insofar as lexicon is concerned, attention has already been called to the use of Latinisms. Besides this element, one also finds numerous Americanisms. Some of these words as *cancha* (Quechua, *maíz tostado*) (*Doc.*, 109) and *guaco (planta americana)* (83) are indigenous to the New World, but others have taken on new regional meanings. *Tasca (oleaje fuerte)* (102), *paporretas (dicho o razón sin ton ni son)* (85), de *pipiripao (de poca importancia)* (85), *bausán (holgazán)* (85), and *mazamorra (especie de gachas de harina de maíz con leche y azúcar o sal)* (90) are all words and phrases used in their respective contexts with regional or American meanings.

Some complexities and deviations from syntactical norms are to be noted in these particular poems as they were in those already discussed. The following is an apt illustration of this: "Del poder la materia efecto ha sido/de toda creación..." (108). The sentence would read with greater facility in prose, "La materia ha sido efecto del poder de toda creación..." Another stylistic feature of Caviedes' syntax which has been noted on other occasions is the large number of modifying adjectives that are employed at times. In the following examples, one sees the use of both ante and postpositioned adjectives in clusters of three and four:

>Te mostraré con razones
>Evidentes, puras, claras. *(Doc., 109)*

>Dizque son unas jeringas
>altas, delgadas y secas... (90)

>es la más común flaqueza
>siempre de inmundas, mundanas,
>profanas, ninfas venéreas... (91)

Aside from these basic elements of style in his syntax, few other pertinent observations can be made on these particular elements in this facet of Caviedes' works. These features are evident, however, not in just these works alone, but in practically all of the poet's production.

It has been noted in the analysis of these seventy poems that a wide variety of subjects and situations are treated. Aside from a few purely lyric works, the majority of them are informative in nature and treat subjects such as death, contemporary happenings, riches and poverty, life in general, and some myths. The principal recurring theme is death, although love is secondary in a few of the works. Since there is a wide variety of subjects, several different theses are found in the works.

The most commonly used form is the sonnet, although the *romance* is employed several times. The *cuartetas, redondillas,* and *quintillas,* which make up the *agudas* and *epigramas,* form the largest single segment of poems in the group. No forms appear here that have not been seen in other facets of the poet's works, nor are there any metrical innovations. Of special interest, as regards interior structure and internal development, is the use of the epistolary form, rhetorical questions, and the dialogue, drama-like poem.

Baroque features of epoch style are found in several different poems. The most salient of these features are seen in examples of *conceptismo, juegos de palabras,* hyperbole, garish imagery, Latinisms, classical allusions, and hyperbaton. Nevertheless, no single poem presents excessive evidence of any one of these characteristics.

Among the other techniques employed most by the author in his poetic art are parallelisms, enumerations, metaphors, visual and auditory imagery, apostrophe, personification, alliteration, and at times internal rhyme. In most cases these are the same rethorical and poetic figures which are found in the other facets of Caviedes' works.

In the lexicon and syntax the most noteworthy elements are the Latinisms and Americanisms, the use of hyperbaton and other syntactical complexities, and the abundance of modifying adjectives which are used at times.

As a group, these works do not represent an important phase of the poet's artistic development. They are in a sense the remnants or miscellany which for one reason or another do not seem to fit into the other groupings of Caviedes' works. This is not to say that they especially lack the artistry of the other works; in fact some of these individual poems are quite worthy of being considered as representative of the author's production. The collection of *agudas* and *epigramas* more than any other single unit does not offer any particular elements which might enhance Caviedes' standing as a poet. In most cases it might be easily imagined that they were nothing more than a few quick verses jotted down by the poet on one occasion or another. Considered as a group, all of these miscellaneous poems present a kind of compendium of the many stylistic devices and techniques that are often found in Caviedes' works, since they undoubtedly represent different stages of the poet's development.

CHAPTER VIII

CONCLUSION AND EVALUATION

As stated at the beginning of this study, the primary purpose has been to determine and describe the general characteristics of Caviedes' poetic art. The total poetic production considered in this study has consisted of two hundred sixty-eight poems. This over-all group has been divided into what seem to be three separate, although somewhat overlapping stages in the poet's artistic development. The fourth division contains those works which for one reason or another do not seem to fit properly into any of the other three groupings.

The initial phase of the poet's development consists primarily of works of an amorous nature. Besides the theme, they are characterized in part by bucolic and rustic situations, pastoral characters, and plaintive, lyric laments. The second period is made up of poetry of social satire. Invectives are directed not only against the members of the medical profession, but also against other professions, types, and women. Many of the characters in these poems are nonfictional, especially the doctors, while practically all of the women are purely creations of the poet's imagination. The third stage which has been discussed is made up of poems of a religious nature. While some are doctrinal, others involve the adoration of God, Jesus Christ, and the Virgin, or present lyric confessions of a sinner. The miscellaneous group of poems has a diversity of subjects which include contemporary happenings, Nature's phenomena, and mythological situations, along with themes treating death, riches, and poverty.

The strophe which predominates over all others in the combined groups is the *romance* of which there are one hundred six. Next in order of frequency of use is the sonnet which appears sixty-six times. The remainder of the poems include *décimas espinelas, seguidillas, pareados, coplas de pie quebrado, endechas reales, glosas, letrillas,* and a single *romance heroico.* Besides poems of *redondillas, quintillas,* and *cuartetas,* there are sixty *epigramas* and *agudas* of a single stanza which use these same forms. The use of the traditional *romance* in the poetry of social satire seems to be a direct reflection of the more popular subject matter of those poems, although its use is not limited to just that one group nor to popular subject matter in Caviedes' works. In contrast, however, the sonnet predominates in the religious poetry which is of a more elevated, aristocratic nature and less popular. It seems to be generally true that Caviedes wrote his best poetry in traditional forms, particularly the *romance.* The vast majority of the sonnets are lacking in general poetic expression and are somewhat prosaic. Most of them have neither the lyric qualities of many of the amorous poems nor the density of thought and intensity of purpose of the satirical works.

The predominant features of epoch style are those of the Baroque, although certain elements akin to the Renaissance are evident, especially in the amorous poetry. The use of *conceptismo, juegos de palabras,* antitheses, certain stylistic *juegos,* hyperbole, and hyperbaton is particularly evident in the poetry of social satire; whereas the religious poetry shows certain elements of *culteranismo,* particularly in the use of *palabras cultas,* allusions, contrasts, and garish imagery. These features would seem to show a gradual artistic and aesthetic development on the part of the poet from an initial period of both renaissance and baroque influences, through the *conceptista* period of the poetry of social satire and into the more *culterano* stage of the religious poetry. The miscellaneous poetry in turn presents a combination of all these features, not so much as a group, but as individual works.

Among the different types of metaphors to be found in the four groups of poems, those which stand out from the rest are the ones used in the satires of doctors and in the religious poetry when referring to God, Jesus, of the Virgin. In the former most are related to death and serve to give emphasis to the thesis that all doctors are murderers. The basic type of imagery utilized in all of these poems is primarily visual, although other sensory imagery is used to a lesser degree. Bucolic and rustic imagery is most commonly found in the amorous poetry, while that of the satirical works reflects much of Caviedes' daily life. In the latter the poet draws on his knowledge of card games, astrology, medical paraphernalia, and implements of war in a vast assortment of different types of images, which also include all sorts of flora and fauna, many of which are indigenous to the New World. The imagery of the religious poetry is generally characterized by its luminous and garish nature in most cases.

Poetic or rhetorical techniques which are utilized in these poems are of a wide variety of types. Chief among those used by Caviedes are parallelism, enumerations, comparisons, personification, alliteration, internal rhyme, onomatopeia, oxymoron, apostrophe, and some symbolism. These techniques are used, however, for different purposes in individual works. In some cases they are utilized as a means of building up the intensity of a specific passage or to add certain sound patterns which augment or emphasize meaning. Although some of these techniques are more commonly encountered in one group of poems than in another, they are all found in varying degrees of frequency in the different facets of the poet's works.

The most salient features of the lexical elements are found above all in the large number of Americanisms, some of which are of indigenous origin, found mainly in the satirical and miscellaneous poems. Other elements that have been noted are the *cultismos* of the religious poetry, a few neologisms, some scatological remarks, and Latinisms taken primarily from Church Latin and medical aphorisms. An analysis of the syntax has shown certain complexities such as long involved sentences and many cases of hyperbaton, although these elements are not found in every poem. Another feature of syntactical style is the use of multiple attributive and descriptive adjectives in some poems.

One gross distortion of the poet's works has been the labeling of a large portion of them as vulgar, nauseating, or lewd. It is true that about three percent of the total works have some remarks which might shock the more modest reader or offend the propriety of others, but it is this very disregard for public censure or the opinions of others on any level that makes many of these poems all the more enjoyable. Had the poet hesitated to express his opinions of others, however biting, the entire effect of a vast majority of his poems would have been lost.

Caviedes' *criollismo* is evident primarily in some of the satirical and miscellaneous works, as some of his critics have suggested. This consists in the main of the mentioning of nonfictional characters, situations, and certain lexical elements which can be related to a specific period of time or environment. Nevertheless, such is not true of the amorous or religious works which are not restricted by any regional qualities. Even in the satires of doctors, it has been noted that a long tradition of such works had preceded those of Caviedes and, although certain elements are regional, they do not warrant the assertion that the poet's most outstanding feature is his *criollismo*. The essence of satire, as seen in these works, is found in the attacks on human faults and frailities which are not limited by time or to a specific place, but are essentially universal.

If one were to pick out the most significant portion of Caviedes' works, it would quite probably be the poetry of social satire. The vehemence of the poet in his attacks on fellow human beings, together with the underlying secondary meanings inherent in the satire, make these works the most significant and important facet of the poet's art. The universal appeal of the humorous situations involved in these poems is one of their prime aesthetic qualities. In many cases this humor arises directly from the double or multiple meanings found in the *conceptismo* and *juegos de palabras*. Other aspects of the poet's works are no less appealing. Such is the case of many of the "Romances amorosos", which would appeal to some through the use of bucolic and rustic imagery, and especially through their lyric nature which involves plaintive amorous laments. The poet's artistry is also quite evident in many of the religious poems, particularly so in the long "Romance a Jesucristo" and the "Letanías de dos esdrújulas a María santísima".

Because of a lack of good editions, most critics have been unable to appreciate adequately the extent and balance of the poet's works. The initial and final periods of amorous and religious poems balance out the author's total production which seems to reach its apex in the poetry of social satire. Even though the satirical works do form the nucleus of his production, it would be unjust to classify Caviedes completely as a satirical poet, since this would imply a complete disregard for his other works.

It is not intended to imply that each of Caviedes' poems has a high level of artistic merit, since many of them lack, among other things, continuity of development or density of thought; however, such is true of any artist's works, especially so in the case of a lay writer such as Caviedes. As is the case of all artistic productions, each work can best be judged individually and then these judgments may in turn be applied to the complete works collectively. Perhaps Caviedes' greatest fault as a poet is that the quality of his works is not consistent.

Caviedes is not now nor will he probably ever be considered as one of Spanish America's foremost poets, but in his own environment and epoch, there were few to surpass him. The universal themes and subjects of which he wrote—love, hate, death, religion, humor, and satire—are elements which can be appreciated regardless of time or place. Caviedes' own particular art of expressing them is above all his primary merit as a poet. It is thus anticipated that in some way this study of his poetic art will lead others to appreciate his works more fully in all of their various facets.

APPENDIX I

Included in this appendix is an alphabetical listing of all the poems written by Caviedes. They have been placed in the appropriate sections corresponding to the groups in which they were analyzed for the study. Those marked with an asterisk are specifically mentioned or textually cited in the study. The *agudas* and *epigramas*, because they lack titles in most cases, are listed by the first verse. Page numbers without a specific text cited are from the *Obras*. Poems taken from the Odriozola edition are cited as *Doc*. Other works which are found only in the MSS are so noted.

I. AMOROUS POETRY

*1.	A dos amigas que se educaban en un monasterio	73
2.	A la ausencia de una dama	MS. Madrid, 291r-292r
*3.	Al amor (epigrama)	207
4.	A los ojos de una dama	MS. Madrid, 247r-248r
*5.	A los ojos de otra dama	MS. Madrid, 248r-248v
*6.	A una dama en el prado	MS. Madrid, 248v-249r
*7.	A una dama en un baño	109
8.	A una dama paseando en un jardín	100
9.	A una dama que lo era del interés	56
10.	A una ingrata	104
*11.	A una dama, jubilada por vieja	108
12.	Aunque Venus no se da (aguda)	MS. Yale-A, 156v
*13.	Coplas (De Menga los ojos)	78
*14.	Da el autor catorce definiciones al amor	MS. Madrid, 294r-294v
*15.	Endechas (Atiende, ingrata Dafne)	77
*16.	En metáfora de ruiseñor explica sus pesares	MS. Yale-B, 101v-102r
*17.	Glosa (Corazón, pues que quisiste)	47
*18.	Pidiendo el alma	48
19.	Remedios contra pensamientos lascivos	100
*20.	Romance amoroso I	61

APPENDIX I   151

*21.	Romance amoroso II	61
*22.	Romance amoroso III	62
*23.	Romance amoroso IV	63
*24.	Romance amoroso V	64
*25.	Romance aomroso VI	65
*26.	Romance amoroso VII	66
*27.	Romance amoroso VIII	66
*28.	Romance amoroso IX	67
*29.	Romance amoroso X	68
*30.	Romance amoroso XI	68
*31.	Romance amoroso XII	69
*32.	Romance amoroso XIII	70
*33.	Romance amoroso XIV	70
*34.	Romance amoroso XV	71
*35.	Romance amoroso XVI	72

II. POETRY OF SOCIAL SATIRE

A. Medical Satire

*36.	Al doctor Bermejo por haberlo hecho rector	93
*37.	Al doctor Corcobado que contestó los versos precedentes con unas décimas y unos esdrújulos tan esdrújulos como él, I, II	Doc., 46 & 47
38.	Al doctor Coto en su casamiento	Doc., 117
*39.	Al doctor Fuentidueñas porque replicando a un grado de bachiller en la Facultad de Matanza dijo que havía vaguidos de estómago	233
*40.	Al doctor Machuca, oponiéndose a la cátedra de venenos, alegó como mérito el ser doncel	Doc., 69
*41.	Al doctor Yáñez que andaba de color y con espada	270
*42.	Al médico malo (epigrama)	206
*43.	Al que leyere este tratado de esta obra: prólogo	214
*44.	A Machuca por su nombramiento de médico de la Inquisición	264
*45.	A un curador de cataratas	297
*46.	A un desafío que tenía dicho corcobado con un cirujano tuerto, sobre salir discordes de una junta	237
*47.	A un doctor de anteojos que pronosticó a una señora que pariría hembra, y ella, por desmentirlo, parió varón	271
*48.	A un hijo de un sastre metido a médico	107
49.	A un médico tuerto con anteojos que desterraron de el Callao, siendo él sólo, porque mataba más que muchos juntos y tenía por flor comerles la comida a los enfermos diciendo que los animaba a comer	268
*50.	A un mulato cohetero que dejó de serlo y se hizo médico	103
*51.	A un médico que se alaba mucho de una curación	Doc., 70
52.	El autor a Cámaras	206
*53.	Aviendo dicho el doctor Yáñez que se disculpaba de no haber hecho segunda visita a un enfermo por vivir fuera de murallas, estando Lima amagada de corsarios	240

*54. Aviendo el doctor Melchor Vásquez avecindádose, después de el temblor, en la calle nueva, los vecinos no le admitieron y le fijaron este edicto en la esquina 263
*55. Aviendo enfermado el autor de tercianas, llamó al médico Llanos a que le curase. Recetóle sangrías, nieve, orchatas y ayudas frescas: hizo lo contrario y sanó. Celébrase en este romance 273
*56. Aviendo hecho el doctor Yáñez en una parroquia de esta ciudad una capilla o sagrario para colocar el Señor, le pidió al author unos versos para que se cantasen el día de la colocación y le envió este romance 242
*57. Aviendo presentado el doctor Machuca un memorial para que se desterrase la semilla de los pepinos, por nociva, se responde lo siguiente 254
*58. Carta que escribió el autor al Dr. Herrera, el tuerto, a quien llevó de esta ciudad a la de Quito el presidente y le hizo protomédico y catedrático de prima del rastro de la medicina 300
*59. Casamiento de Pico de Oro con una panadera vieja, viuda y rica 266
*60. Causa. Presentóse esta petición ante el Sr. Don Juan de Caviedes, juez pesquisidor de los errores médicos, en Lima, a 9 de marzo de 1690, contra un médico que, a sustos, quiso matar al Dr. Martín de los Reyes 288
*61. Causa que se fulminó en el parnaso contra el doctor Vásquez por haberle tirado un carabinazo a otro médico, en un muladar 279
*62. Coloquio que tuvo con la Muerte un médico estando enfermo de riesgo 230
63. Copla de el autor 213
*64. Dedicatoria a la muerte 222
*65. Efectos del protomedicato de Bermejo escripto por el alma de Quevedo 305
66. Epitafio en el sepulcro de la mujer de Pico de Oro 273
*67. Fe de erratas 213
*68. La fruta del Paraiso (aguda) 205
*69. Loa a Utrilla, por la curación que hizo de un potro a una dama con la felicidad de que no murió en la cura 247
*70. Loa en aplauso del Dr. Francisco Machuca por haver curado a una prima del autor y averla muerto como a todos los que cura 259
*71. La medicina continua (aguda) 202
*72. Memorial que da la muerte al Virrey (Duque de la Palata) en tiempo que se arbitraba enviar navíos y gente para pelear con el enemigo o si se construía muralla para guardar esta ciudad de Lima 250
*73. Parecer que da de esta obra la anatomía del Hospital de San Andrés 217
74. Pedro es doctor sin rival (aguda) 205
75. Por el author, redondilla a Pedro 246
76. Por D. Lorenzo, médico indiano 247

*77.	Pregunta que hacen los alguaciles y escribanos, temerosos de que se les pegue a los gatos la peste de los perros	303
*78.	Que teman a los temblores y no teman los doctores	292
*79.	Representación de unos comerciantes quiteños contra el doctor Herrera	298
*80.	Respuesta de la Muerte, I, II	225 & 226
*81.	Romance jocoserio o a saltos al asunto que el dirá, si lo preguntasen los ojos que quisieren leerlo	312
82.	Si yo pierdo la salud (aguda)	203
*83.	Vejamen que le dió el author al zambo Pedro de Utrilla, el mozo, haviendo sacado una piedra a una mujer y se corone con un rodete de malvas, por laurel, con esta copla	243

B. SATIRE OF OTHER PROFESSIONS AND OF TYPES

*84.	Al casamiento de Pedro de Utrilla	248
85.	Al demonio y a los que lo imitan	186
86.	Al dicho corcobado porque se puso espada luego que sucedió el terremoto de octubre de 1687	237
*87.	Al guarda del comercio de Lima que rodó de un techo ...	192
88.	Al mismo asunto de este casamiento	160
*89.	Al mismo asunto en arrimados	162
*90.	Al mismo asunto en lengua de indio	161
91.	A otro narigón	105
92.	A un abogado narigón	104
*93.	A un abogado que dejó de serlo para hacerse médico	278
*94.	A un amigo que tenía una yegua muy flaca y pequeña	189
*95.	A un amigo viejo en su cumpleaños	175
*96.	A una persona grave que vestía de negro y era amigo de negras	178
97.	A un avariento (epigrama)	207
98.	A un corcobado hojalatero que se casó con una mujer muy alta y le dieron en dote unas arrobas de plomo	159
*99.	A un corcobado que casó con una mujer larga dotada en plomo (epigrama)	210
100.	A un desafío que tuvieron los corcobados Liseras y Mejía ...	109
101.	A un hombre pequeño, viejo y rico que casó con moza arrogante y pobre	Doc., 193
102.	A un marido sufrido que su mujer vestía y sustentaba	107
*103.	A un mulato que decía que de él había aprendido, cuando iba a verlo	208
*104.	A un narigón disforme	MS. Madrid, 207v-210v
*105.	A uno que preciaba mucho de poeta, por haberlo sido su madre	167
106.	A uno que tenía muchos libros (epigrama)	209
*107.	A un pintor que retrataba a una dama y la miraba con anteojos	52
*108.	A un poeta disparado que andaba recitando sus versos que dedicaba a quien se lo pagaba	165
*109.	A un poeta que de hacer versos le dieron seguidillas ...	Doc., 137

°110.	Aviendo escrito el excmo. Sr. Conde de la Monclova un romance, los ingenios de Lima lo aplauden en muchos y el poeta en este romance	36
111.	Conjuraba a una mujer endemoniada un exorcista tonto y presumido de poeta y el autor le aconseja lo que ha de hacer en estas coplas	174
°112.	Cuatro contras que ha de tener el entendido para serlo	106
113.	Dándole a Pedro de Utrilla el parabién de un hijo que le nació	103
°114.	Haviendo cobrado doce pesos el canónigo capón de la limosna de unas misas en huevos, le salieron hueros, suceso que dió asunto a este romance ... ... MS. Madrid, 224r-225v	
°115.	Habiéndole vestido su excelencia ilma. le dió este segundo memorial en agradecimiento	154
116.	Habiéndose graduado de doctor un abogado muy pequeño y flaco, escribió el autor este romance	170
117.	Maestro sin barba y bobo (aguda)	205
°118.	Memorial de los mulatos para representar una comedia al Conde de la Monclova, en ocasión de haber quitado a uno de la horca	163
119.	Memorial que dió un borracho al arzobispo pidiéndole un vestido de los doce que da en el lavatorio del Jueves Santo, en este romance	153
120.	Memorial que dió un corcobado al virrey, pidiendo soltura para un hermano suyo zapatero, sentenciado a Chile ...	173
°121.	Memorial que dió un representante al Sr. Virrey en ocasión que había de representar en palacio la comedia de Tetis y Peleo	156
°122.	Para labrarse fortuna en los palacios	96
123.	Para ser cavallero	96
124.	Pasaba un chivato capitaneando unos corderos	105
°125.	Pintura de un borracho gracioso	157
°126.	Pintura de un borracho que se preciaba de poeta	146
127.	Pregón	181
°128.	Quintillas en el certamen que se dió por la Universidad, a la entrada del Conde de la Monclova. Fue un coloquio que dos pobres de las gradas tubieron, celebrando la abundancia de mantenimientos que con su govierno havía y llorando la esterilidad de tiempos pasados	40
°129.	Receta que el poeta le dió a Liseras para que sanase de la giba, I, II	276 & 277
130.	Remedio para lo cavalleresco	96
°131.	Remedios para ser lo que quisieres	129
132.	Romance (Los curas encubridores)	262
133.	Sátira segunda (epigrama)	209
134.	Sátira tercera (epigrama)	210

C. Feminine Satire

°135.	A la bella Arnarda	Doc., 134
°136.	Al casamiento de un viejo escribano	Doc., 209

137.	A una dama pedigüeña (epigrama)	210
*138.	A una dama que cayó de la mula en que iba a Miraflores	MS. Madrid, 117v-120r
*139.	A una dama que estaba amancebada con un mercader capón	MS. Yale-B, 98v-99v
*140.	A una dama que por serlo con demasía la prendieron.	Doc., 216
*141.	A una dama que por serlo paró en la Caridad	Doc., 126
*142.	A una dama que rodó del Cerro de San Cristóval	Doc., 213
*143.	A una dama que se ajustaba los pies	184
*144.	A una dama que se sacó una muela por dar a entender que las tenía	208
145.	A una dama sumamente pedilona	94
*146.	A una fea	210
147.	A una mojigata (epigrama)	206
*148.	A una vieja del Cuzco, grande alcahueta y revendedora de dos hijas, mestizas como ella, le escribió este romance. ...	166
149.	A una vieja que habiendo sido dama paró en ser alcahueta ...	109
*150.	A un mozo pobre que casó con una mujer vieja, fea y rica.	179
151.	Cara la mujer se advierte (aguda)	205
*152.	No teme Paula al francés (aguda)	202
*153.	Otro a la misma, usando el trueco de ambos abusos de el fingido embuste	196
*154.	Pintura de una dama en metáfora de astrología	45
*155.	Pintura de una dama en seguidillas	49
*156.	Pintura de una dama que con su hermosura mataba como los médicos	53
*157.	Pintura de una fea buscona en metáfora de guerra, en coplas de pie quebrado	169
*158.	Una pintura en metáfora de los naipes	50
*159.	Retrato de una beldad limense, usando de el común embuste de los patricios de esta ciudad	195
*160.	Romance alevoso a las seguidillas de una dama	Doc., 129
*161.	Siendo hueso la mujer (aguda)	202
*162.	Todas las mujeres mandan (aguda)	201
*163.	Tu frente es desnuda y fría (aguda)	203
164.	Vendes tu amor y es fingido (aguda)	202

III. RELIGIOUS POETRY

*165.	A Cristo	24
*166.	A Christo crucificado	23
*167.	Acto de contrición	13
168.	A Dios sacramentado	31
*169.	Adoración al santísimo sacramento, traducida del ritmo de Santo Tomás de Aquino	22
*170.	A la asumpción de María santísima	26
*171.	A la concepción de María santísima	31
*172.	A la cruz en que murió Cristo	29
*173.	Al conmoverse la naturaleza en la muerte de Christo	26
*174.	Al conocimiento de Dios y la criatura	27
*175.	Al misterio de la encarnación	24

*176.	A lo que el entender humano alcanza de los juicios divinos.	29
177.	A María santísima, empieza y acaba con título de comedia.	20
*178.	A San Antonio Abad ...	25
*179.	A San Miguel ...	30
*180.	Como debe estar el moribundo católico, dirá este soneto ...	28
*181.	Consejos para los mandamientos de la ley de Dios ...	17
*182.	Consuelo de poderosos y felices ...	25
*183.	Convida a los doctos theólogos al reparo de las materias de decreto ...	97
184.	Del sacro fuego, arcaduz (aguda) ...	204
*185.	Letanías de dos esdrújulas a María santísima ...	8
186.	Otro (Tanto siento el haberos ofendido) ...	23
187.	Otro (Vos, muerto en una cruz porque yo viva) ...	25
*188.	Para saber el enojo de Dios ...	30
*189.	Pidiendo perdón a Dios el alma arrepentida ...	23
*190.	Porqué dejó Dios su creencia a la fe y no a la evidencia ...	28
*191.	Por qué razón nace la sabiduría del temor de Dios ...	29
192.	Prueba que se ve a Dios más patente, que cuando al hombre le parece que no hay Dios ...	27
193.	Quicumque de S. Atanasio ...	10
*194.	Reconviniendo la misericordia de Dios ...	27
*195.	Romance a Jesucristo ...	1
*196.	Salve glosada para la natividad de María santísima ...	16

IV. MISCELLANEOUS POETRY

197.	A dos padres lindos que tuvieron un hijo feo (epigrama) ...	206
*198.	A la muerte del Duque de la Palata a quien mató su médico en Portovelo con sangría de tobillo ...	105
*199.	A la muerte del Maestro Baes ...	58
200.	Al cabrón (epigrama) ...	207
*201.	Al mismo asunto del muelle ...	103
*202.	Al muelle acabado ...	102
*203.	Al muelle que hizo en el Callao Monclova ...	102
204.	Al sepulcro del Duque de la Palata ...	106
*205.	Al terremoto acaecido en Lima el 20 de octubre de 1687 ...	79
*206.	Al terremoto que asoló esta ciudad ...	95
*207.	A mi muerte próxima ...	295
208.	Apolo a Cámaras (epigrama) ...	206
209.	A un caballero ingenioso a quien el autor visitó queriéndole pagar la visita lo repugnó y apurándole respondió este soneto ...	110
210.	Aunque mi madre y mi padre (aguda) ...	201
*211.	Bola es el mundo que sola (aguda) ...	203
212.	Caerá el que en contemplaciones (aguda) ...	204
*213.	Carta que escribió el autor a la monja de México, habiéndole ésta enviado a pedir algunas obras de sus versos, siendo ella en esto y en todo el mayor ingenio de estos siglos.	32
214.	Casados (epigrama) ...	206
*215.	Coloquio entre la vieja y Periquillo sobre una procesión celebrada en Lima ...	83

°216.	Como debe ser el juez para ser bueno	101
217.	Compra, si quieres tener (aguda)	203
218.	Con las armas del dinero (aguda)	202
219.	Contentos falsos de esta vida	98
220.	Cosa nueva en esta edad (aguda)	204
221.	Creció de aplauso al compás (aguda)	205
222.	El dar publicando es golpe (aguda)	201
°223.	Defensa de un pedo ... ... Doc.,	109
224.	Define la vida de los hombres	99
°225.	Definición a la muerte	95
226.	Definición de lo que es ciencia	99
227.	De hierro frío a ser pasa (epigrama)	207
228.	Después de abrasada Troya (aguda)	202
229.	Dios de los libros te libre (aguda)	204
230.	Dos veces para mi santo	212
°231.	En la muerte de mi esposa	78
°232.	Fábula burlesca de Júpiter e Io	147
233.	Ha venido a convencerme (aguda)	204
234.	Jácara	44
°235.	Juicio del cometa	190
236.	Licencia del ordinario de las damas	214
°237.	Lo que son riquezas del Perú	98
238.	El mayor enemigo que un hombre tiene es a sí mismo	97
°239.	Narciso y Eco	197
°240.	No hay cosa cierta en esta vida	99
241.	Obra de tinieblas es (aguda)	205
242.	Otro al mismo asunto. Jocoso.	101
243.	Para morir mucho importa (aguda)	204
244.	La piedra que buscas, Pedro (aguda)	202
°245.	Polifemo y Galatea	117
246.	Por qué al recivir, o al dar (aguda)	201
247.	Primero, antes que la lengua (aguda)	203
248.	Privilegio	214
°249.	Privilegios del pobre	211
°250.	Que los temblores no son castigo de Dios	108
°251.	Que no hay más felicidad en esta vida que el entendimiento.	110
252.	El que ve el mal en aquel (aguda)	204
°253.	Razón porqué los pobres son capaces y los ricos torpes	101
254.	Redondillas ortográficas	116
°255.	Remedio para ser rico	107
°256.	La riqueza es más desgracia que dicha	98
257.	Si a la templanza el desorden (aguda)	205
258.	Si como en un muro, en mí (aguda)	203
259.	Siempre repite el ser largo (aguda)	202
260.	Si la cabeza es simpleza (aguda)	203
261.	Si te faltasen corderos (aguda)	201
262.	Son la cama y el sepulcro (aguda)	205
263.	Tasa	213
264.	Ut, re, mi, fa, la alegre (aguda)	201
°265.	Yo solo sé que no sé (aguda)	203

APPENDIX II

Included in this appendix are descriptions of the eight known MSS of Caviedes' works. In order to facilitate their identification in the accompanying study of Caviedes' poetry, they have been given the arbitrary titles of MSS. Duke, Madrid, Molíns, Ayacucho, Yale-A, Yale-B, Lima-A, and Lima-B, according to their locations and present owners.

1. MS. DUKE. This MS is by far the most complete of the seven manuscripts consulted. The MS is composed of one volume with the texts of the works being contained in the initial two hundred eighty-six folios. At the end is an unnumbered and incomplete index of six pages. The frontispiece consists of a typewritten note, inserted at the beginning by its old owner Francisco Pérez de Velasco, which reads as follows:

> El Sr. Ricardo Palma, en una incorrecta edición, según el mismo, dio a conocer las producciones de Caviedes [*Documentos literarios del Perú,* Vol. V]. En 1899 las publicó de nuevo, según el manuscrito de Cipriano Coronel Zegarra. El presente tiene más de 60 sonetos no publicados y otras composiciones inéditas. Las precede una composición en verso que no sé si fue escrita por Caviedes u otro aficionado a las musas. Lima, Marzo 29 de 1908.

Eight unnumbered pages follow the frontispiece and contain unidentified verses which do not seem to belong to Caviedes. Written in a different hand from that of the rest of the MS, they are almost illegible.

The title page of the work reads as follows:

> Guerra fisica, proezas medicales, hazañas de / la ignorancia, sacadas a luz de el conocimiento por / un enfermo, que milagrosamente escapo, de los errores / medicos por la proteccion de Sr Sn Roque abogado contra / medicos, o contra la peste, que tanto monta. Dedicalo su / author a la muerte emperatriz de medicos, a cuyo augusto palido cetro, / le feudan vidas, y tributan saludes en / el thesoro de muertos y enfermos.

Following this on the same page are the "Aprobación" and a "Copla". The MS contains two hundred eleven of the two hundred sixty-eight poems which can be attributed to Caviedes and is composed of the works contained in the *Diente del Parnaso* as well as *poesías diversas*. Also included are three *bayles* or *entremeses* which appear in but three of the other MSS (Madrid, Molíns, and Ayacucho). The most notable absences are the "Romances amorosos" (found primarily in MSS. Yale-A and Lima-B) of which only two of sixteen are included. Twenty-six of the works not found in MS. Duke are *agudas* and *epigramas*, which are predominantly found in other MSS. According to Vargas Ugarte in his "Introducción" to the *Obras* (p. XXI), the handwriting seems to correspond to about the first third of the eighteenth century. The MS is presently found in the Duke University Library and carries the signature: 146. Peruvian Collection. No. 913.

2. MS. MADRID. This MS, although not so complete as MS. Duke, undoubtedly owes its origin to the same or a very similar source. It contains one hundred eighty-eight of the total known poems, or in a comparison with MS. Duke, some twenty-three less than the latter. Most of the basic omissions are the same, notably the "Romances amorosos", some of the religious poems, and a large number of *agudas* and *epigramas*. The frontispiece reads only "Poesías de Juan del Valle Caviedes". The title page of the MS consists of the following:

> Guerra Phisica, proezas medicales, o / hazañas de la ignorancia, sacadas a luz / del conocimiento por un enfermo, que mi- / lagrosamente escapo de los errores me- / dicos por la proteccion del Señor San Ro- / que abogado contra medicos, o contra / la peste, que tanto

monta. Dedicalas / su autor a la muerte, emperatriz de / medicos, a cuyo augusto palido cetro / feudan vidas, y tributan saludes en el / thesoro de muertos, y enfermos.

This is then followed by the "Aprobación" and two "Coplas". The title, of course, refers to the *Diente del Parnaso* which has a similar title page in all the MSS. The single volume is composed of three hundred forty-three folios, plus twelve pages of a complete index. As in the case of MS. Duke, the three bayles form a part of the works included. According to Vargas Ugarte the handwriting is more modern than that of MS. Duke and is probably from the last third of the eighteenth century ("Introducción", p. XXI). Although not so complete, a close examination of some of the poems has showed it to be more accurate in many cases than MS. Duke. MS. Madrid was acquired by the Biblioteca Nacional de Madrid from the Colección Gayangos and carries the signature 17494 of that library.

3. MS. MOLINS. This MS consists of a single volume and is presently in the private collection of don W. Jaime Molíns of Buenos Aires. A copy of the entire MS has not yet been consulted, but the owner has graciously provided microfilm of portions of the work and a complete index of its contents.

The frontispiece of the MS contains the following information:

DIENTE DEL / PARNASO / Que trata diversas materias, contra / Medicos, de Amores, a lo Divino / Pinturas, y Retratos. / Compuesto por Don Joph. [sic] Cabiedes / Que escribio en Lima / Ano de 1689.

The title page consists of the following:

Gueras [sic] Fisicas, Proezas Medicales/azanas de la ygnorancia, sacadas a luz / de el conosimiento, por un Emfermo que milagrosamente escapo de los herrores medicos por la proteccion de el Glorioso Senor / San Roque a Vogado [sic] contra Medicos, o contra la / Peste, que tanto monta.

Also included on the title page are a "Dedicatoria", an "Aprobación", and an octosyllabic "Copla de el Autor a el Asumpto".

The third page of preliminaries consists of another *copla* and the "Fe de erratas" which is written in the form of a *romance*.

The corpus of this MS is made up of two hundred sixty pages of text of which only the first eighty are numbered consecutively. The one hundred fifty poems, thirty-eight less than MS. Madrid, contained in this MS are arranged in both single and double columns in what seems to be a single hand, possibly that of a scribe from the first half of the eighteenth century. Also included in the MS are three dramatic works. Two of these, the *Baile entremesado del amor alcalde* and the *Baile del amor tahur* appear in other MSS. The third, however, appears solely in this source and without a doubt was not written by Caviedes. It is a kind of jocular *entremés* and is entitled *Mojiganga para festejar Los años del Rey nuestro Señor*. The play was written in honor of Luis I of Spain, who reigned for only seven months after Philip V abdicated in January, 1724, thus making it postdate Caviedes' death by a quarter of a century.

4. MS. AYACUCHO. A first-hand description of MS. Ayacucho cannot be given, since all attempts to acquire microfilm of the work have not been successful. Luis Fabio Xammar, in an article published in the *Boletín de la Biblioteca Nacional* in Lima (October, 1944, p. 7), was the first to describe the MS after learning of its existence during a trip to Ayacucho in 1944. The title page reads the same as that of MS. Madrid and seems to contain the same basic works as MSS. Duke, Madrid, and Molíns, among them being two of the three *bayles* already mentioned. It is probably related to all of the previously mentioned manuscripts. Whether it is as complete as the others cannot be proved just at this point. According to Xammar the MS consists of one volume and is composed of one hundred three folios without an index or date. The signature corresponding to the MS is 15/176 of the Biblioteca del Convento Franciscano de Ayacucho.

5. MS. YALE-A. This was one of two MSS that were acquired by that university's library in October, 1912. According to notes found on the inside of the cover, it was bought by the members of the Hiram Bingham expedition from a Lima bookseller, Francisco Pérez de Velasco. MS. Yale-A is one of the MSS that has evidently never been consulted for any of the editions made of

Caviedes' works to date. The frontispiece of the MS reads as follows:

> *Diente del Parnaso* / que trata dibersas mate- / rias contra medicos, ver- / sos amorosos, a lo divino, / pinturas, y retratos. / Compuesto / Por don Juan Cabiedes. / que escribio en / Lima / Año de 1689.

The title page is very similar to those of the previously described MSS with a few differences as one may see in the following:

> Guerras fisicas, proezas / medicinales, hazanas de la / ignorancia, sacadas a luz / del conocimiento por un enfer- / mo, que milagrosamente es- / capo de los errores medicos / por la proteccion del glorioso S. / Roque, abogado contra / medicos o contra peste, que / tanto monta. Dedicalo su autor a la / muerte emperatriz de / medicos, a cuyo augusto / cetro le feudan vi- / das, y tributan saludes en el / tesoro de muertos, y enfer- / mos.

The volume consists of two hundred fourteen folios of text, an unnumbered index of eight pages, and like MS. Molíns contains one hundred fifty poems. Conspicuously absent are most of the religious poems and those of a philosophical nature, as well as the dramatic pieces. All but a few of the numerous *agudas* and *epigramas* are found in this MS.

6. MS. LIMA-B. From all available information, this MS has never been consulted for an edition either. It was among the works which were salvaged from the Biblioteca Nacional de Lima after the edifice was destroyed by a catastrophic fire on May 10, 1943. Much of the exterior of the MS was burned by the fire and blurred by water, but luckily it is possible to identify every poem contained in it. From the legible portions of the frontispiece, it can be verified that it is unquestionably the same as that of MS. Yale-A, since it bears the same wording and date of 1689. A partially legible note in another hand at the bottom of the page mentions the edition made by Odriozola and Palma, as well as the latter's *Flor de Academias y Diente del Parnaso*. The note might very well have been made by Palma who was the Biblio-

teca Nacional's librarian from 1883 to 1912, since another note at the end of the MS, which reads as follows, is signed by Palma:

> Esta copia es detesta- / ble. Léase a Caviedes / en el tomo V de *Do-* / *cumentos literarios del Perú,* por Odriozola / la edición que aunque / no es muy correcta, / por lo menos vale más que / este manuscrito. / [Signed] Palma. (121v).

The title page of the MS is essentially the same as that of MS. Yale-A. With the exception of eight omissions, MS. Lima-B contains the same poems as MS. Yale-A. In all it has one hundred forty-two poems contained in one hundred twenty-one folios. An unnumbered index at the end consists of four pages.

7. MS. YALE-B. MS. Yale-B was also acquired from Francisco Pérez de Velasco in October, 1912, by the Hiram Bingham Expedition. Like MS. Yale-A it has evidently never been consulted for any of the editions made to date. The title page of the MS is completely missing with the text beginning on page one, which contains two sonnets, the "Definición de lo que puede ser la muerte" and "A Christo crucificado". The text is contained in one hundred thirty-six folios followed by seven unnumbered pages of index. Since it does not list any poems before the two previously mentioned, it may be assumed that the original text is intact except for the preliminary pages. Of all the known MSS, this is the least complete. It contains only one hundred four poems, the majority of which are from the *Diente del Parnaso*. A future collation of this MS and MS. Lima-A will undoubtedly substantiate the proximity of their relationship.

8. MS. LIMA-A. This MS was acquired by the Biblioteca Nacional de Lima by donation from the Librería Internacional del Perú after the previously mentioned fire. It had originally belonged to the private collection of Dr. Hermilio Valdizán. It contains one hundred five poems or one more than MS. Yale-B. The frontispiece is in block print and reads as follows:

> COPIA PERFECTA / SI PERFECCION / CAUE EN TAL CO- / PIA DE LOS MEDI- / COS DE LIMA. SV / AVTOR DON JV- / AN CAUIERES [sic] / JVES

164   THE POETIC ART OF JUAN DEL VALLE CAVIEDES

PESQVISA- / DOR DE LOS DES- / ACIERTOS MEDI- / COS / ANO DE 1690.

The title page from this MS is also missing. The text is contained in one hundred twenty-four folios plus eight unnumbered pages of index. Following the index are four more numbered folios bearing the title "Dibersas Poesías del mismo Autor que se han hallado / después descrito este" (125r-128r). This section contains five poems, one of which has only the initial lines of the text and is marked out, and the "Salve glosada" which is the only poem not found in MS. Yale-B. One other identifying feature is found in a note by a hand different from that of the text which says. "Soy de don Agustín Menéndez Valdés" (9r). All attempts to identify this person have thus far been unsuccessful. This was one of the MSS consulted by Vargas Ugarte for his 1947 edition of the poet's works.

The existence of still other MSS has been mentioned by several different writers. Odriozola in the 1873 edition states that he used a MS which had belonged to Dr. José Manuel Valdés, a Lima physician. The editor does not describe the MS, but a comparison of what he published with the known MSS shows it to be most like MSS. Yale-A and Lima-B. Palma, in the prologue to that edition, says that the MS was a copy made in 1691 and describes it as being so faded as to be almost undecipherable. This MS subsequently disappeared and its whereabouts are still unknown.

In 1899 Palma obtained and published in his *Flor de Academias y Diente del Parnaso* a MS which belonged to the private library of D. Cipriano Coronel Zegarra. This is the only mention of the MS and its whereabouts are also unknown. From a comparison of Palma's 1899 edition with the existing MSS, it seems to have been most like MSS. Yale-B and Lima-A.

Ricardo Palma also mentioned the existence of yet another MS. In the "Prólogo muy preciso" of the 1873 edition he says:

> En 1859 tuvimos la fortuna de que viniera a nuestro poder un manuscrito de enredada y antiguo [sic] escritura. Era una copia, hecha en 1693, de los versos que,

bajo el mordedor título de *Diente del Parnaso* escribió por los años de 1683 a 1691 un limeño mercader nombrado D. Juan del Valle y Caviedes (p. 5).

In the same prologue Palma adds that the MS was subsequently stolen, but only after he had examined a biographical note on Caviedes which it contained. This MS has evidently not come to light since Palma last saw it, as no one else has ever mentioned seeing a MS with any biographical notes. It has also been noted by Ricardo Palma in this same prologue that a bibliophile, don Gregorio Beeche of Valparaiso, owned a MS of Caviedes' works in 1862, and that the libraries of Buenos Aires, Mexico City, and Bogota had assured him that they also possessed other MSS; however, none of these seems to have been rediscovered to the present time.

LIST OF WORKS CONSULTED

ALONSO, DÁMASO. *La lengua poética de Góngora*, RFE, Anejo XX (1935), 97-108.

———. *Góngora y el 'Polifemo'*. Madrid, 1960.

ANDERSON IMBERT, ENRIQUE. *Historia de la literatura hispano-americana*. 2 vols. 3rd. ed. Mexico, 1961.

ANDERSON IMBERT, ENRIQUE and EUGENIO FLORIT. *Literatura hispanoamericana. Antología e introducción histórica*. New York, 1960.

ANONYMOUS. "Fotoduplicados de manuscritos y libros raros", *Boletín de la Biblioteca Nacional*, IV (June, 1947), 221-231.

———. "Los diarios de Lima en el 1er. aniversario del incendio de la Biblioteca Nacional", *Boletín de la Biblioteca Nacional*, I (July, 1944), 291-298.

ARONA, JUAN DE. *Diccionario de peruanismos*. Paris, 1938.

ARROM, JOSÉ JUAN. *Estudios de literatura hispanoamericana*. La Habana, 1950.

BARREDA Y LAOS, FELIPE. *Vida intelectual de la colonia*. Lima, 1909.

BEARDSLEY, MONROE C. *Aesthetics: Problems in the Philosophy of Criticism*. New York, 1938.

BERMEJO Y ROLDÁN, FRANCISCO. *Discvrso/de la enferme-/dad del sarampión expe-/rimentado en la civdad de los Reyes del Peru/Por/el Doc. D. Francisco, BERMEJO, Y ROL/DÁN, Cathedratico de Prima en la facultad de Medi-/cina, Prothomedico general de estos Reynos, y Me-/dico de Cámara del Excelentissimo, e/Ilustrissimo Senor Doctor Don Melchor/ de Linan, y Cisneros, del Excmo. Senor Conde de la Monclova Comendador de la/Zarza en el Orden, y Cauallería de Alcantara, del Consejo de/Guerra de su Magestad, y Iunta de guerra de Indias, Virrey/ Gouernador, y Capitan General de estos Reynos y/Prouincias del Peru, Tierrafirme, Chile*, &c. Lima, 1694. In Hermilio Valdizán. *Apuntes para la bibliografía médica peruana*. Lima, 1928, pp. 29-39.

BROOKS, CLEANTH AND ROBERT PENN WARREN. *Understanding Poetry*. New York, 1960.

BURKE, KENNETH. *The Philosophy of Literary Form*. New York, 1957.

BURNSHAW, STANLEY et al., eds. *The Poem Itself*. New York, 1960.

CÁCERES SÁNCHEZ, LETICIA. *La personalidad y obra de D. Juan del Valle y Caviedes*. Lima (unpublished thesis), 1944.

CARILLA, EMILIO. *El gongorismo en América*. Buenos Aires, 1946.

———. *Quevedo, entre dos centenarios*. Tucumán, Argentina, 1949.

———. "Restituciones a la lírica española", RFH, VIII (1946), 148-150.

CHAMPION, EMILIO. *La obra poética de Juan del Valle y Caviedes y su influencia en el criollismo peruano.* Lima (unpublished thesis), 1953.

———. "Nota biográfica de Caviedes", *Letras*, V (1939), 98-103.

———. "Picardía de Caviedes", *3 (Tres)*, no. 4 (March, 1940), 50-56.

COSSÍO, JOSÉ MARÍA DE. *Fábulas mitológicas en España.* Madrid, 1952.

Diccionario de literatura española. 2nd ed. Madrid, 1953, pp. 727-728.

EGUIGUREN, LUIS A. *Catálogo histórico del claustro de la Universidad de San Marcos (1576-1800).* Lima, 1912.

GALT, WILLIAM R. "Life in Colonial Lima", *Hispania*, XXXIII (August, 1950), 247-250.

GARCÍA CALDERÓN, VENTURA. *Biblioteca de cultura peruana*, 12 vols. París, 1938.

———. "La literatura peruana (1535-1914)," *Revue Hispanique*, XXXI (1914), 305-391.

GUTIÉRREZ, JUAN MARÍA. "Don Juan Caviedes, fragmento de unos estudios sobre la literatura del Perú", in *Documentos literarios del Perú*, ed. Manuel de Odriozola, Lima, 1873, V, 9-20.

———. *Escritores coloniales americanos.* Ed. Gregorio Weinberg. Buenos Aires, 1957.

HESPELT, E. HERMAN et al., eds. *An Anthology of Spanish American Literature.* New York, 1946.

JOHNSON, HARVEY L. "Review of Kolb: *Juan del Valle y Caviedes*", *Hispanic Review*, XXIX (April, 1961), 162-163.

JUANA INÉS DE LA CRUZ, SOR. *Obras completas de Sor Juana Inés de la Cruz: Villancicos y letras sacras*, II, ed. Alfonso Méndez Plancarte. Mexico, 1952.

KAYSER, WOLFGANG. *Interpretación y análisis de la obra literaria*, trans. M. D. Mounton and V. G. Yebra, 2nd ed. Madrid, 1958.

KOLB, GLEN L. *Juan del Valle y Caviedes. A Study of the Life, Times and Poetry of a Spanish Colonial Satirist.* New London, Connecticut, 1959.

LAPESA, RAFAEL. *Historia de la lengua española*, 4th ed. New York, 1959.

LASTRES, JUAN B. *Historia de la medicina peruana: La medicina en el virreinato*, II. Lima, 1951.

LAVALLE, J. A. AND DOMINGO DE VIVERO. *Galería de retratos de los gobernadores y virreyes del Perú.* Barcelona, 1909.

LEONARD, IRVING A. "Caviedes, José Hernández, and the 'Under Dog' a Parallelism", *Hispania*, XXXIII (February, 1950), 28-29.

LOHMANN VILLENA, GUILLERMO. "Apuntaciones sobre el arte dramático en Lima durante el virreinato", *3 (Tres)*, no. 7 (December, 1940), 28-57.

———. *El arte dramático en Lima durante el virreinato.* Madrid, 1945.

———. "Dos documentos inéditos sobre don Juan del Valle y Caviedes", *Revista Histórica*, IX (1937), 277-283.

———. "Una poesía autobiográfica de Caviedes inédita", *Boletín Bibliográfico de la Universidad Nacional Mayor de San Marcos*, XIV (June, 1944), 100-102.

———. "Un poeta virreinal del Perú: Juan del Valle Caviedes", *Revista de Indias*, no. 33-34 (1948), 771-794.

MARTÍNEZ DE CUÉLLAR, JUAN. *Desengaño del hombre en el tribunal de la fortuna y casa de descontentos*, ed. Luis Astrana Marín. Madrid, 1928.

MEDINA, JOSÉ TORIBIO. *La imprenta en Lima (1584-1824).* 2 vols. Santiago, 1904.

MENDIBURU, MANUEL DE. *Diccionario histórico-biográfico del Perú.* 8 vols. Lima, 1874-1890.
MENÉNDEZ Y PELAYO, MARCELINO, ed. *Antología de poetas hispanoamericanos,* III. 2nd ed. Madrid, 1894.
MERCEDES MÁRQUEZ, DOLORES DE LAS. "Un poeta limeño del siglo XVIII [sic] Caviedes y 'El Diente del Parnaso'", *Histonium,* año VII, no. 94 (1947), 151-153.
──────. "Trasunto de Calderón en el 'Poeta de la Ribera'", *Histonium,* año IX, no 97 (1947), 379-381.
MIRÓ QUESADA, AURELIO. "La literatura del Perú virreinal", *El Comercio* (Sept. 9, 1953), 2.
MONTERO DEL ÁGUILA, DIEGO. *Oracion/Panegyrica/Qve al primer feliz ingresso del/Excelentissimo Senor Don Melchior Portocarrero/Lasso de la Vega, Conde de la Monclova Comendador de/la Zarza, del Orden de Alcantara, del Consejo de Guerra, y Iunta de Guerra de Indias, Virrey, Governador, y/Capitan General que fue del Reyno de Mexico,/actual que es destos Reynos del Peru,/Tierra-firme, y Chile, &c./En la Real Vniversidad/de S. Marcos de la Ciudad de los/Reyes. Corte del Peru/El favsto dia 30 de Octubre/del Ano de 1689./Dixo/El Doctor D. Diego Montero del/Aguila Abogado de la Real Audiencia, y del Fisco, y/presos del Santo Oficio de la Inquisicion de/este Reyno, Cathedratico de Prima de Leyes en la mesma Vniversidad./Y consagra reverente./A la excelentissima Senora Dona Antonia Ximenez de Vrrea, Clavero, y Sessè, Condesa,/de la Monclova, &c. Virreyna del Perú,/Tierrafirme, y Chile, &c.* Lima, 1689. In José Toribio Medina, *La imprenta en Lima (1584-1824).* Santiago, 1904, II, 180-181.
MOYA, ISMAEL. *Romancero general.* 2 vols. Buenos Aires, 1941.
MS. Duke (microfilm). Duke University Library.
MS. Lima-A (microfilm). Biblioteca Nacional de Lima.
MS. Lima-B (microfilm). Biblioteca Nacional de Lima.
MS. Madrid (microfilm). Biblioteca Nacional de Madrid.
MS. Molíns (microfilm). Private library of don W. Jaime Molíns, Buenos Aires.
MS. Yale-A (microfilm). Yale University Library.
MS. Yale-B (microfilm). Yale University Library.
NAVARRO TOMÁS, TOMÁS. *Métrica española, reseña histórica y descriptiva.* Syracuse, 1956.
Nuevo pequeño Larousse ilustrado, trans. Miguel de Toro y Gisbert, 34th ed. Buenos Aires, 1959.
ODRIOZOLA, MANUEL DE. "Advertencia oportuna", in *Documentos literarios del Perú,* ed. Manuel de Odriozola. Lima, 1873, V, 3-4.
OROZCO DÍAZ, EMILIO. *Temas del barroco.* Granada, 1947.
PALMA, RICARDO. "Prólogo", in *Flor de Academias y Diente del Parnaso,* ed. Ricardo Palma. Lima, 1899, p. 335.
──────. "Prólogo muy preciso", in *Documentos literarios del Perú,* ed. Manuel de Odriozola. Lima, 1873, V, 5-8.
PAZ SOLDÁN, CARLOS ENRIQUE. *Cuatro siglos de medicina limense.* Lima, 1935.
PAZ SOLDÁN Y UNÁNUE, PEDRO. *Diccionario de americanismos.* Lima, 1884.
PETSCH, ROBERT. "El análisis de la obra literaria", in *Filosofía de la ciencia literaria,* trans. Carlos Silva. México, 1946, pp. 251-292.
POLLOCK, THOMAS CLARK. *The Nature of Literature.* Princeton, 1942.

Picón-Salas, Mariano. *De la conquista a la independencia*. Mexico, 1944.
Prado, Javier. *El genio de la lengua y de la literatura castellana y sus caracteres en la historia intelectual del Perú*. Lima, 1918.
Prince, Carlos. *Bosquejo de la literatura peruana colonial*. Lima, 1910-11.
Quesada, Vicente G. *La vida intelectual en la América española durante los siglos XVI, XVII y XVIII*. Buenos Aires, 1917.
Reedy, Daniel R. "Poesías inéditas de Juan del Valle Caviedes", *Revista Iberoamericana*, XXIX (1963), 157-190.
Richards, Ivor Armstrong. *Practical Criticism*. London, 1929.
Riquer, Martín de. *Resumen de la versificación española*. Barcelona, 1950.
Rivera Serna, Raúl. "Índice de los manuscritos existentes de la Biblioteca Nacional", *Boletín de la Biblioteca Nacional*, IX (December, 1952), 95-172.
Rodríguez-Navas y Carrasco, Manuel. *Diccionario general y técnico hispanoamericano*, 2nd ed. Madrid, 1919.
Romero, Emilia. *El romance tradicional en el Perú*. Mexico, 1952.
Romualdo, Alejandro and Sebastián Salazar Bondy, eds. *Antología general de la poesía peruana*. Lima, 1957.
Sánchez, Luis Alberto. *La literatura del Perú*. Buenos Aires, 1939.
―――. *La literatura peruana*. 6 vols. Asunción, Paraguay, 1950-51.
―――. *Los poetas de la colonia y de la revolución*. Lima, 1947
―――. "Un Villón criollo", *Revista Iberoamericana*, II (April, 1940), 79-86.
Santamaría, Francisco J. *Diccionario general de americanismos*. 3 vols. Mexico, 1942.
Shipley, Joseph T., ed. *Dictionary of World Literature*. Patterson, New Jersey, 1960.
Sigüenza y Góngora, Carlos de. *Libra astronómica y filosófica*, ed. Bernabé Navarro. Mexico, 1959.
Sotomayor y Mogrobejo, Ismael. "Juan del Valle y Caviedes, autor colonial peruano vinculado a la historia literaria boliviana", *La Prensa* (Lima, June 13, 1943), 8.
Tagle, José G. *Los culteranos en el Perú*. Lima, 1942.
Tamayo Vargas, Augusto. *Literatura peruana*. 2 vols. Lima, 1953.
Tauro, Alberto. *Bibliografía peruana de literatura, 1931-1958*. Lima, 1958.
Torres-Ríoseco, Arturo. *The Epic of Latin American Literature*. New York, 1942.
Unánue, Hipólito. "Rasgos inéditos de los escritores peruanos", *Mercurio Peruano*, I (April 28, 1791), 312-313.
―――. "Rasgo de nuestro anti-galeno Caviedes", *Mercurio Peruano*, II (June 12, 1791), 3.
Valdizán, Hermilio. *Apuntes para la bibliografía médica peruana*. Lima, 1928.
―――. *La facultad de medicina en Lima*. Lima, 1944.
Valle Caviedes, Juan del. "Conversación que tuvo con la muerte un médico estando enfermo de riesgo", *Mercurio Peruano*, V (July 5, 1792), 152.
―――. *Defensa que hace un pedo al ventoso: por don Juan Caviedes, mercader de Lima. Dedícala a los autores y consortes de cierto manifiesto un extranjero, layco, mercader de libros, que apenas los conoce por el rótulo para venderlos*. Lima, 1814.

VALLE CAVIEDES, JUAN DEL. *Diente del Parnaso*, eds. Luis Alberto Sánchez and Daniel Ruzo. Lima, 1925.

———. *Diente del Parnaso. Poesías serias y jocosas*. In *Documentos literarios del Perú*, ed. Manuel de Odriozola. Lima, 1873, V, 21-281.

———. *El amor alcalde. Bayle cantado del amor médico. Bayle de el amor tahur*. Lima, 1953.

———. "Flor de leer, 'Lamentaciones sobre la vida en pecado'", *Mar del Sur*, VIII (Sept.-Oct., 1952), 80-81.

———. *Obras de Don Juan del Valle y Caviedes*, ed. Rubén Vargas Ugarte. Lima, 1947.

———. "Respuesta de la muerte al médico en este romance", *Mercurio Peruano*, V (July 8, 1792), 156.

———. *Romance, en que se procura pintar, y no se consigue: La violencia de dos terremotos, con que el poder de Dios asoló esta Ciudad de Lima, Emporeo de las Indias occidentales, y la más rica del mundo*. Lima, 1688. In José Toribio Medina, *La imprenta en Lima (1584-1824)*. Santiago, 1904, II, 178-179.

VALLE CAVIEDES, JUAN DEL et al. *Flor de Academias y Diente del Parnaso*, ed. Ricardo Palma. Lima, 1899.

VARGAS UGARTE, RUBÉN. *Biblioteca peruana: manuscritos peruanos en las bibliotecas del extranjero*. 9 vols. Lima, 1937.

———. *Glosario de peruanismos*. Lima, 195-.

———. *Historia del Perú: virreinato (siglo XVII)*. 2 vols. Buenos Aires, 1954.

———. "Introducción", in *Obras de Don Juan del Valle y Caviedes*, ed. Rubén Vargas Ugarte. Lima, 1947, pp. VIII-XXIV.

VILANOVA, ANTONIO. "Las fuentes y los temas del 'Polifemo' de Góngora", *RFE*, Anejo LXVI (1957), II, 805-872.

WELLEK, RENÉ "The Concept of Baroque in Literary Scholarship", *Journal of Aesthetics and Art Criticism*, V (1946), 77-109.

WELLEK, RENÉ AND AUSTIN WARREN. *Theory of Literature*. New York, 1949.

WIESSE, CARLOS. "Literatura colonial", *Revista Universitaria*, III (Sept., 1909), 509-525.

WIMSATT, WILLIAM KURTZ Jr. *The Verbal Icon*. Lexington, Kentucky, 1954.

XAMMAR, LUIS FABIO. "Dos bayles de Juan del Valle y Caviedes", *Fénix, Revista de la Biblioteca Nacional*, no. 2 (1945), 277-285.

———. "El terremoto en la literatura peruana", *3 (Tres)*, no. 6 (Sept., 1940), 43-56.

———. *La poesía de Juan del Valle y Caviedes en el Perú colonial*. Lima, 1946.

———. "La poesía de Juan del Valle y Caviedes en el Perú colonial", *Revista Iberoamericana*, XII (1947), 75-91.

———. "Un importante manuscrito de Juan del Valle Caviedes", *Fénix, Revista de la Biblioteca Nacional*, no. 3 (1945), 629-631.

———. "Un manuscrito de Juan del Valle Caviedes en la Biblioteca Nacional, I", *Boletín de la Biblioteca Nacional*, I (July, 1944), 373-374.

———. "Un manuscrito de Juan del Valle Caviedes en la Biblioteca Nacional, II", *Boletín de la Biblioteca Nacional*, II (October, 1944), 7.

———. "Veintitrés sonetos inéditos de Juan del Valle Caviedes". *Fénix, Revista de la Biblioteca Nacional*, no. 3 (1945), 632-641.

www.ingramcontent.com/pod-product-compliance
Lightning Source LLC
Chambersburg PA
CBHW021844220426
43663CB00005B/398